MORMON MISSION PREP

A Practical Guide to Spiritual
and Physical Preparation

BY JAMES R. SMITH

Dedication:
To my children. May this book help prepare you for your missions.

Appreciation:
I thank my wife Heather for putting up with me and all the time I put into this book and into the website. I also thank my editors, Terry, Paul, and Heather; your feedback has made the book much better than it would be otherwise. And, most especially, I thank my Lord and Savior Jesus Christ for giving me the inspiration, strength, and determination to complete this project.

ISBN-13: 978-0-9836059-0-4
Library of Congress Control Number: 2011906825

Cover Photograph: Wheat by Flickr user jayneandd

"For behold the field is white already to harvest; and lo, he that thrusteth in his sickle with his might, the same ... bringeth salvation to his soul." D&C 4:4

Table of Contents

Guide to Using this Book

This book is divided into five sections.

Section 1. The Desire: In this first section, I discuss why every young man, and some young women, should serve a mission. The Lord needs you, the Church needs you, and you need the spiritual growth and life experiences that a mission will bring.

Section 2. The Papers and Process: This section explains the mission application process, the timeline of when to begin the process, and the details of the mission paperwork. I also talk about the mission call letter and packet of materials and how every mission call comes from God.

Section 3. Temporal and Physical Preparation: In this section I discuss the financial cost of a mission and give some advice on saving money. I share ideas about what to bring on your mission, and I give tips for young people living on their own for the first time.

Section 4. How to Become an Effective Missionary—The Spiritual Preparation: Though much of the other sections of the book discuss the spiritual aspects of mission prep, this section focuses on it more directly. In this section I discuss worthiness requirements, how to use the scriptures, and other ways to access the Spirit of the Lord to teach effectively.

Section 5. Additional Blessings of Missionary Work: In this last section I talk about temple marriage preparation and other blessings that flow from faithful missionary service.

If you are a youth and your mission is still a year or more away...you may want to skim Section 2. This section covers the mission papers and the application process. Once the time to leave on your mission gets closer, a year or six months away, then return and reread these chapters in their entirety.

If you are a youth and your mission is less than a year away...start at the beginning and read the whole book through. May it help prepare you to be a more effective missionary, be a better representative of the Lord, and bring more souls unto Christ.

If you are a parent or leader of a youth...you'll also want to read the book in its entirety so you can be aware of the mission application and call process, as well as the tips for physical and spiritual missionary preparation.

You'll find more up-to-date and detailed information on missionary preparation including videos and links to helpful Church articles on my website, www.MormonMissionPrep.com.

Introduction

"Give me a young man who has kept himself morally clean and has faithfully attended his Church meetings. Give me a young man who has magnified his priesthood and has earned the Duty to God Award and is an Eagle Scout. Give me a young man who is a seminary graduate and has a burning testimony of the Book of Mormon. Give me such a young man, and I will give you a young man who can perform miracles for the Lord in the mission field and throughout his life" (Ezra Taft Benson, "To the 'Youth of the Noble Birthright," Ensign, May 1986, 45).

This book is an outgrowth of a website I felt inspired to start back in 2008 called MormonMissionPrep.com. I have felt the Lord's promptings and guidance in developing the website and in writing this book. I'd like to tell you a little about how these projects came to be.

In January of 2008, I began working for the LDS Church. My job was to work with the Web analytics of Church websites. During that first year I had a spiritual prompting that would not go away that I should build a website about Mormon missionary preparation. I had always felt that I had many wonderful experiences as a missionary in Argentina, so building a website to share those made sense. I did some research and couldn't find any mission prep websites out there on the Internet. I thought, then, that I should do what I could to help future missionaries to be better prepared to serve the Lord on their missions.

In early 2009, I started the MormonMissionPrep.com website. I anticipated using the site to share my mission stories and to write articles about preparing spiritually to be one of the Lord's servants to bring the gospel to all the earth. While the site has certainly been that, something happened as I began running the website that I did not expect: I began to get email after email from youth and parents asking questions about the more practical aspects of mission preparation. I received many questions about spiritual aspects of mission prep as well, but more often I have found people were looking for information about the mission paperwork and application forms, the call process and timeline, qualifications, how to repent, what to bring, how much to save, and so on.

As I reflected back on my own pre-mission experiences, the need for these practical mission prep tips made sense. When I was a freshman at Brigham Young University (BYU), filing mission papers and sharing your mission call was a frequent topic of conversation and even ward activities. Many of my fellow freshman didn't know when or how to begin the process of applying for a full-time mission. We other practical concerns like if we should go through the application process in our home ward or student ward (you can do it either way, though I'd recommend using your home ward).

It has now been over two years since I started MormonMissionPrep.com. These past two years have given me ample experience in the questions and issues facing pre-missionaries and their families. I have greatly enjoyed receiving many emails and comments from young people and their families. I have done much analysis of the traffic to the site, and I have chosen material for the book from the most popular topics on the website.

This book is relatively short, just over 100 pages, and should not be too difficult for most teenagers and pre-missionaries to read. You'll see me refer often to my website for more detailed information. I do this because there simply isn't enough room to put everything mission prep-related in this book. Like the prophet Mormon, I feel like I "cannot write the hundredth part of the things" that are in my heart (see The Words of Mormon 1:5). But in the future and as I have time, I will put as many mission prep resources as I can on MormonMissionPrep.com.

In writing articles for the website, and now as I write this book, I'm gearing my advice and recommendations primarily to young men and young women, but also to their parents and leaders. I hope this book will provide that much needed guidance in the practical areas of mission preparation.

Throughout the book I will also touch on aspects of spiritual preparation and the divine blessings of missionary work. There is no more important work that you can be engaged in than sharing the restored gospel of Jesus Christ. As the Lord told John Whitmer in D&C 15:6: "Behold, I say unto you, that the thing which will be of the most worth unto you will be to declare repentance unto this people, that you may bring souls unto me, that you may rest with them in the kingdom of my Father."

I know that as you young people prepare yourselves in all aspects, both physical and spiritual, you will become more effective instruments in the hands of the Lord. We are led by a living prophet, and The Church of Jesus Christ of Latter-day Saints truly is the Lord's Church. Your mission call comes from God through inspired priesthood leaders. Honor that call. Represent the Lord and His Church well. And by so doing you will be blessed beyond measure in this life and the next.

Section I.   The Desire

Chapter 1   Deciding to Serve a Mission

"What we need now is the greatest generation of missionaries in the history of the Church. We need worthy, qualified, spiritually energized missionaries who, like Helaman's 2,000 stripling warriors, are "exceedingly valiant for courage, and also for strength and activity" and who are "true at all times in whatsoever thing they [are] entrusted" (Alma 53:20). (M. Russell Ballard, "The Greatest Generation of Missionaries," October 5, 2002)

Before you can prepare for a mission, you will first need to decide to go on a mission. For some of you, that decision will be relatively easy: your father, mother, brother or other family member or close friend went on a mission and set the example for you. Or perhaps you were raised in the Church and you've known since you were a little boy that when you turned 19 you'd be going on a mission. Or perhaps you are a young man or young woman who simply feels a burning desire to go on a mission.

For others, the decision to serve a mission will be more difficult. In the LDS Church culture it is expected, almost as a rite of passage, for young men to serve a mission, but you may not have that desire. Some of you may have other priorities: a girl friend, schooling, a job, or an athletic career.

The decision to serve a full-time mission is deeply personal, but I hope you make the choice to go. Let me assure you that there is no priority more important in the eternal scheme of things than for you young men to serve a mission when you reach age 19. By serving a mission you will bring eternal blessings upon those you meet, upon your family, and upon yourself.

To you young men who haven't made the determination to prepare and serve a mission, don't procrastinate as it will only make it harder to come to the right decision. Make the decision now to keep yourself worthy and to serve a full-time mission. It will bring a positive change to your life forever.

I am grateful that you are reading this book. As I tell about my mission experiences, I hope you feel the joy serving a mission brought me. A mission will do the same for you and, in the process, you will do immeasurable good for other people. The Lord needs you to be a missionary!

Every Young Man Should Serve a Mission

Most of you have probably heard that, in the LDS Church, we expect every worthy young man to fulfill a mission. This is not new, every prophet since President Spencer W. Kimball, 12th president of the Church, has repeated that charge. Prior to President Kimball, the Church had a large missionary program and many young men and young women served missions. But the expectation that every young male member should prepare and serve a mission wasn't quite as strong then as it is today.

In 1974, President Kimball gave a landmark address that changed the way Latter-day Saints view the missionary service of young men. Thomas S. Monson, then a member of the Quorum of the Twelve Apostles, said President Kimball's talk "had profound and deep influence on all who heard it." Elder Monson further said that "the impact of his dynamics as a missionary-oriented person…have set in motion factors which have resulted in one of the greatest upsurges in missionary work that we have ever seen" (Status Report on Missionary Work, Ensign, October 1977).

This is what President Spencer W. Kimball said:

"The question has been often asked, Is the mission program one of compulsion? And the answer, of course, is no. Everyone is given his free agency. The question is asked: Should every young man fill a mission? And the answer of the Church is yes, and the answer of the Lord is yes. Enlarging this answer we say: Certainly every male member of the Church should fill a mission, like he should pay his tithing, like he should attend his meetings, like he should keep his life clean and free from the ugliness of the world and plan a celestial marriage in the temple of the Lord" (Spencer W. Kimball, "Planning for a Full and Abundant Life," Ensign, May 1974, 86).

Since President Kimball's memorable address, every prophet of the Lord has repeated that message, that every worthy, able young man should serve a mission. The prophet and president of the Church after President Kimball was Ezra Taft Benson, and this is what he said:

"The Lord wants every young man to serve a full-time mission. Currently, only a fifth of the eligible young men in the Church are serving full-time missions. This is not pleasing to the Lord. We can do better. We must do better. Not only should a mission be regarded as a priesthood duty, but every young man should look forward to this experience with great joy and anticipation. What a privilege—what a sacred privilege—to serve the Lord full time for two years with all your heart, might, mind, and strength.

You can do nothing more important. School can wait. Scholarships can be deferred. Occupational goals can be postponed. Yes, even temple marriage should wait until after a young man has served an honorable full-time mission for the Lord." (Ensign, May 1986, pp. 44–45).

Howard W. Hunter was the 14th President of the Church, and this is what he said:

"Earlier prophets have taught that every able, worthy young man should serve a full-time mission. I emphasize this need today" (Howard W. Hunter, "Follow the Son of God", Ensign, Nov. 1994, 87).

Gordon B. Hinckley, our 15th prophet and Church President said:

"I throw out a challenge to every young man within this vast congregation tonight. Prepare yourself now to be worthy to serve the Lord as a full-time missionary. He has said, 'If ye are prepared ye shall not fear' (D&C 38:30). Prepare to consecrate two years of your lives to this sacred service. That will in effect constitute a tithe on the first twenty years of your lives" (Conference Report, Sept.– Oct. 1995, 70; or Ensign, Nov. 1995, 51–52).

Our prophet today, President Thomas S. Monson, has repeated the call:

"I repeat what prophets have long taught—that every worthy, able young man should prepare to serve a mission. Missionary service is a priesthood duty—an obligation the Lord expects of us who have been given so very much. Young men, I admonish you to prepare for service as a missionary. Keep yourselves clean and pure and worthy to represent the Lord" (President Thomas S. Monson, "As We Meet Together Again," October 2010).

Sisters Serving Missions

While this book is more closely targeted to young men, young women who desire to prepare for and serve a mission will also greatly benefit from reading it. I'd like to just briefly mention what our two most recent prophets have said about sister missionaries:

"Regarding single sisters serving as missionaries: We need some young women. They perform a remarkable work. They can get in homes where the elders cannot. But it should be kept in mind that young sisters are not under obligation to go on missions. They should not feel that they have a duty comparable to that of young men, but some will wish to go. If so, they should counsel with their bishop as well as their parents" (Gordon B. Hinckley, To the Bishops of the Church, Worldwide Leadership Training).

"A word to you young sisters: while you do not have the same priesthood responsibility as do the young men to serve as full-time missionaries, you also make a valuable contribution as missionaries, and we welcome your service" (President Thomas S. Monson, As We Meet Together Again, Oct. 2010).

If you are a young woman, please visit
http://www.mormonmissionprep.com/sister-missionaries.
This page is dedicated to sister missionary prep and contains
advice for young women considering serving a mission.

Young Men: We Need You and The Lord Needs You

If you decide to serve a mission simply because the prophets have asked you to as a young man, that is fantastic and you will be blessed for it. If you have a testimony that what the prophets have asked you to do is what the Lord wants you to do with your life, you are to be commended for your faith and diligence. If you want to serve because you love the Lord and you love your fellow beings on this earth and want to bring them the blessings of the gospel, that's even better.

No matter what your reason for serving a mission, start now to prepare to be the best missionary you can be. A prepared missionary is someone who is a humble servant of the Lord. A prepared missionary is someone who will be an instrument in the hands of the Lord in bringing souls unto Christ and building up God's kingdom.

In addition to realizing the duty of young men to serve a mission, know that your service is wanted and needed. This knowledge that the Lord needs can increase your desire to serve.

Not too long ago, I was home teaching and I taught a lesson on the importance of every young man serving a mission. I asked the 16-year-old boy in the family if he planned to serve a mission. He said yes, he was planning to go on a mission, but he said he wasn't sure about a certain friend of his in the ward. If he were placing odds, he said there was only a "20% chance" that his friend would serve a mission.

When I heard that my heart sunk. I felt like there had to be more I could do to help people like this young man in my ward feel the desire to serve a mission. As I was pondering how to motivate young men to have the desire to be a missionary, I happened to read a talk by Elder

M. Russell Ballard of the Quorum of the Twelve Apostles. In it, he was speaking to the youth of the Church, and said:

"We need you. Oh, how the Lord needs you! ... My plea to you this morning for leadership has never been more critical in The Church of Jesus Christ of Latter-day Saints than it is today. I now understand abundantly why the prophets have said that the Lord reserved for this last day some of his very choice spiritual sons and daughters. I understand why you have been reserved to come forth now: because he needs you. He needs you desperately in the building of his kingdom." (M. Russell Ballard, "You—the Leaders in 1988," Ensign, Mar. 1979, 69–73)

Elder Ballard's words rang true to me as a message of motivation for young men to serve a mission. Young men, WE NEED YOU! The world needs you and the message of the gospel of Jesus Christ you will bring. The Church needs you, your goodness, and your leadership. The Lord needs every one of you to be a full-time missionary.

The Harvest is Great but the Laborers are Few

In the New Testament, we read that "the Lord appointed other seventy also, and sent them two and two before his face into every city and place, whither he himself would come. Therefore said he unto them, The harvest truly is great, but the labourers are few" (Luke 10: 1-2).

Young men, the harvest is great! There is no greater blessing that you can bring to people than the message of the restored gospel of Jesus Christ. The population of the earth is approaching 7 billion people, most of whom do not have knowledge of the gospel. A great many of those are honest and good people waiting to hear the message that only true servants of the Lord can bring. Modern revelation confirms this:

"For there are many yet on the earth among all sects, parties, and denominations, who are blinded by the subtle craftiness of men, ... and who are only kept from the truth because they know not where to find it" (D&C 123:12).

Spiritual Starvation that Missionaries Can Alleviate

In 1975, Spencer W. Kimball gave a talk in which he referred to the scripture Amos 8:11: "Behold, the days come, saith the Lord God, that I will send a famine in the land, not a famine of bread, nor a thirst for water, but of hearing the words of the Lord." Then President Kimball said:

"We need to prepare all within our homes to serve beyond our homes as calls and opportunities come to provide leaven for the world. The world wants and needs what we have. In the beautiful prayer by Brother Holland, he mentioned the famine in the world— famine not of bread, not of the ordinary needs, but a famine for the word of the Lord; and you are the custodians of the bread of life, you take it to your families so that they can share it with the people of the world" (Spencer W. Kimball, Men of Example, an address to CES religious educators, 12 September 1975).

Missionaries bring the bread and water of life, the gospel of Jesus Christ, to a world that is dying of spiritual thirst and starvation. There is no greater joy than to teach the gospel to a family that is hungry to know the truths of eternity. As a missionary, you will have many such opportunities.

The Worth of Souls

Jesus said the greatest commandment is to love God and the second greatest is like unto it, to love your neighbors (see Matthew 22: 36-39). Perhaps the best motivation you can have to serve a mission is because you love God and want to obey his commandments and because you love your fellow beings and want to help them.

"Remember the worth of souls is great in the sight of God;... And if it so be that you should labor all your days in crying repentance unto this people, and bring, save it be one soul unto me, how great shall be your joy with him in the kingdom of my Father! And now, if your joy will be great with one soul that you have brought unto me into the kingdom of my Father, how great will be your joy if you should bring many souls unto me!" (D&C 18: 10, 15-16) yan Richards, in the October 1998 General Conference,

octrine that will change the behavior of our young men regarding missions is understanding the worth of a single soul. Jesus Christ paid the supreme sacrifice in providing the infinite Atonement, which provides the only way for us to return and live with our Heavenly Father. When parents, bishops, and our young men understand this true doctrine, our young men will be prepared and have a desire to serve" (H. Bryan Richards, "As for Me and My House, We Will Serve the Lord," October 1998).

As Elder Richards indicated, the Savior loves all of us and understands our eternal value as children of God. "Greater love hath no man than this, that a man lay down his life for his friends" (John 15:13). Because of the Savior's great love for us, He drank the bitter cup, suffered for our sins, and died on the cross. He "suffered these things for all, that they might not suffer if they would repent" (D&C 19:16). When young men truly understand that doctrine, they will have the desire to share that message with the world, go wherever the Lord would have them to go, and bring souls unto Christ.

Young men, please realize how much the Lord needs you to prepare for and serve a faithful full-time mission. And please realize how much the people of the world need you. As you watch the news and see the events of the world, you will notice that crime is rampant. Family values and people's morals continue to decline, and the influence of Satan seems to keep growing. The answers to all of life's problems are in the gospel of Jesus Christ. The key to lasting happiness in this life and the next is to follow the teachings of our Savior. Young men and women who rise up and answer the call to be missionaries can help gather the harvest, show people the way to eternal joy, and help bring Heaven Father's children back into His presence.

Section II.   The Papers and Process

Chapter 2   Overview of the LDS Mission Call Process

"We can all be committed, and this commitment must lead to action. Whether we find ourselves walking eight hours and fording streams in Sunday clothes to attend a priesthood meeting, or putting aside a lifelong goal in order to serve a mission, the Lord sees and blesses those who act on their devotion to him" (M. Russell Ballard, "The Power of Commitment," New Era, Nov. 1989, 4).

Your missionary preparation can and should start early in life. The earlier the better. So it may seem a little strange to begin a mission prep book with the mission call process which you'll begin only a few months before you leave. Let me explain why this is important.

Future missionaries, along with their parents and leaders who may read this book, need to understand the mission application process from start to finish. Understanding this process will help you see where you need to go and how to get there. Understanding this process will help you in short-term and long-term mission preparation. Leading off the book with this subject also seems appropriate because in two years of running the Mormon Mission Prep website, this is the topic I have found to be of most interest to future missionaries and their families.

In the later half of the book, I will spend considerable time on the spirituals aspects of becoming an effective missionary. But in this and the other chapters in this section, I'll be giving a general overview of the mission application papers and process.

Before the Paperwork

First, let's briefly discuss the spiritual and physical preparation you need to do before you start the paperwork to apply to go on a mission. You can prepare spiritually for your mission by studying the gospel personally, with your family, and at Church. Read the scriptures, especially the Book of Mormon, and seek a witness from the Lord of its truthfulness. Pray daily, and seek to gain a personal testimony of the Savior, His Atonement, the restored Church, Joseph Smith, and our living prophet today.

You can begin to prepare temporally and physically from an early age as well. Start as soon as you can to save your money, in a piggy bank or a bank account, whichever you prefer. Look for ways to earn money, then pay 10% as tithing, and save as much of the rest as you can for your mission. Stay physically fit, be active, and keep the Word of Wisdom. Watch your weight and be sure to address any health problems. Missionary work is physically rigorous, so do all you can to keep your body in good shape so you can "run and not be weary." Also avoid or remove any obstacles such as unpaid debts and legal issues.

The Application Process

To begin the application process, the first thing to do is meet with your bishop or branch president. At least four months before you're able to leave on your mission, set an appointment to meet with your bishop for a personal interview. He will give you the information you need to log on to the online missionary recommendation system or he will give you the paperwork if the online system is not available in your area.

The *Missionary Online Recommendation System*, https://apps.lds.org/recentry/login.lds, is the website used by priesthood leaders and candidates to process the full-time missionary application.

18

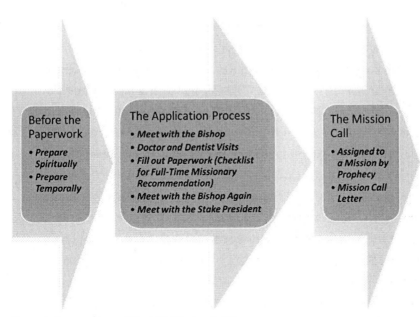

Figure 1: An overview of the LDS Mission Call Process

The next steps, as well as those I will discuss in the next two chapters, are based on the official Church paperwork, the Checklist for Full-Time Missionary Recommendation form, as it stands in 2011. Some of the steps may be changed by the Church in the future, and in such case you should follow the up-to-date instructions in the official Church paperwork.

After having that initial meeting with your bishop, the next thing you need to do is arrange doctor and dentist visits. The paperwork contains medical forms that they will need to fill out. Make appointments with your doctor and dentist as soon as possible because if there are any health or dental issues, like needing wisdom teeth removed, you will have to get them attended to before you leave.

The next step in the application process is to fill out the Missionary Candidate Information section of the paperwork. There are actually several sections of personal information in this part that you will need to complete. You'll fill out background information about yourself, including your desire and ability to learn a language, your schooling, and how your mission will be financed.

As part of the paperwork, you'll have to submit a photograph of yourself. Make sure that in this photo you are dressed and groomed according to missionary standards. This means wearing a suit and tie and having a short haircut for young men, and female equivalent conservative hair and clothing styles for young women. See the Missionary Dress and Grooming Guidelines posted on mtc.byu.edu for more detail. You may also want to go ahead and get a passport photo at this time and use that same photo on your mission application. Additionally, it wouldn't hurt to begin the process of getting a passport at this time. Getting a passport can be a lengthy process and you may want to have one, whether or not you end up going to foreign country on your mission.

Finally, when all the paperwork is filled out and all the medical forms are complete, meet with your bishop or branch president again. You may need to talk to your ward executive secretary to set up this appointment. Bring all the completed forms with you so your bishop can review the application. He will conduct a thorough interview to determine your worthiness, ability to serve, and your testimony of the Savior and the restored gospel. After your interview with the bishop, he will tell you how to set up an appointment with the stake president. Your bishop and stake president will complete some additional parts including their own written recommendations for your missionary service. This is the final step before the application is sent to Church headquarters, either by mail, which a stake leader usually does, or by electronic online submission.

Receiving the Mission Call

Mission calls are made by prophecy and revelation from the Lord. Your mission application will be received by Church headquarters and processed. You will be assigned to a specific mission by a member of the Quorum of the Twelve Apostles, who has been authorized to do so by the president of the Church. Your mission assignment comes only after much prayer, revelation, and confirmation from the Spirit. We'll talk more about how missionaries are called by God later.

Next, Church headquarters will mail you the highly anticipated mission call letter. After the mission call is made, you will get a packet with information on your assigned mission, the date to report to the Missionary Training Center (MTC), a list of specific items you should bring with you, and other necessary information.

Each Call Is Inspired

Though there are a lot of mechanical steps to go through in the process of filling out your mission papers, it's important not to lose sight of the spiritual: the spiritual preparation by the missionary and the spirit of revelation in the issuing of the mission call. Here is what President Henry B. Eyring said about the inspiration of each mission call:

> "I have had [many] experiences feeling of the Holy Ghost...But I've never felt what I have felt as I have...participated in the assigning of missionaries...Because of technology, it is possible for us to have your picture and the information about you displayed. And then quickly, on that same screen, all the missions of the Church with all of their needs are displayed. Within minutes, and sometimes less than a minute, the impression comes so powerfully that it would be, if it were a single instance, something that you would never forget. Can you imagine sitting there for hours at a time, having that happen time after time without interruption? I testify to you that it is real...[The Lord] somehow not only knows you but loves you enough to ensure that your call is where He needs you to go to teach the children of our Heavenly Father." (Pres. Henry B. Eyring, "Called of God," address delivered at the Missionary Training Center, Aug. 26, 1997).

Brothers and sisters, receiving your mission call is a special event. Cherish it. I know your call comes from God, but if you have any doubts, you have the right and the responsibility to go to the Lord in prayer and find out for yourself. There is a scripture in Moroni 10: 4 that you will use frequently in teaching the missionary lessons. It says that through prayer and by the power of the Holy Ghost you can know the truthfulness of the Book of Mormon. Applying this scripture to your mission call, you also can come to know that it came from the Lord. To paraphrase:

> And when ye shall receive [your mission call], I would exhort you that ye would ask God, the Eternal Father, in the name of Christ, if these things are not true; and if ye shall ask with a sincere heart, with real intent, having faith in Christ, he will manifest the truth of it unto you, by the power of the Holy Ghost.

With a personal witness that the Lord Himself sent you to your specific mission, you will be able to go forward with more faith and confidence. You will conduct yourself with dignity and respect for the mission rules. You will work diligently and have success, whether it be planting gospel seeds or harvesting through baptism, according to the will of the Lord. And you will bless the lives of the people you meet, and reserve wonderful eternal blessings for yourself.

I'll Go Where You Want Me to Go

One of my favorite missionary hymns was written by a woman named Mary Brown. Though she was not a Latter-day Saint, her words express the faithful commitment of followers of Christ:

> It may not be on the mountain height
> Or over the stormy sea,
> It may not be at the battle's front
> My Lord will have need of me.
> But if, by a still, small voice he calls
> To paths that I do not know,
> I'll answer, dear Lord, with my hand in thine:
> I'll go where you want me to go.
> I'll go where you want me to go, dear Lord,
> Over mountain or plain or sea;
> I'll say what you want me to say, dear Lord;
> I'll be what you want me to be.
> ("I'll Go Where You Want Me to Go," Hymns, no. 270)

When you submit your mission papers, you indicate your willingness to serve as a missionary for the Lord wherever he, through his living prophet, sends you. Our Savior Jesus Christ gave the greatest example of willingness to go where Heavenly Father wants us to go. The Savior did not want to drink from the bitter cup and suffer for our sins in Gethsemane and on the cross of Calvary (see D&C 19:18). But He, in all humility, said to the Father, "Not my will, but thine, be done" (Luke 22:42).

May we follow the example of Christ, and seek the will of the Father, and not our own. May we, through our words and deeds, always "go where you want me to go, dear Lord." Truly, missionaries are called by God, and through faithful service, they and their families will be greatly blessed of the Lord.

Chapter 3   Details on the Application Forms

"I am asking for missionaries who have been...trained through the family and the organizations of the Church, and who come to the mission with a great desire. I am asking ... especially that we train prospective missionaries much better, much earlier, much longer, so that each anticipates his mission with great joy" (Spencer W. Kimball, "When the World Will Be Converted," Ensign, Oct. 1974, 3).

Let's take a closer look at the paperwork and dive into the details of the application forms. This will provide necessary and important information for missionaries going through this process. If submitting your application is a year or more away, you may want to skim this chapter. Then refer back to this section later when you are going through the mission application process.

The mission application form, or the "Checklist for Full-Time Missionary Recommendation" as it is called by the Church, is the official paperwork you will need to fill out when applying to go on a mission. You can get the application papers from your bishop or branch president, and he will help you through the application process. You may also have the ability to submit your paperwork online through the Missionary Online Recommendation System. If that online system is available, your bishop will advise you on how to use it.

Whether you fill out the physical paperwork, or complete the application online, the form has eight major sections:

1. Missionary Recommendation
2. Priesthood Leaders' Comments and Suggestions

3. Education and Service of Missionary Candidate
4. Unit Information for Missionary Candidate
5. Personal Health History of Missionary Candidate
6. Physician's Health Evaluation
7. Dental Evaluation for Missionary Candidate
8. Personal Insurance Information of Missionary Candidate

1. Missionary Recommendation

The first section of the mission application form is where you provide basic information such as your name, address, and other contact information. You attach a photograph of yourself dressed according to missionary dress standards, fill in your birth date, confirmation date, and any criminal record you might have. You are asked for your citizenship information and residency documents, if applicable. You will also need to provide the name, occupation, and contact information of your parents, or caregiver if you live with someone other than your parents.

2. Priesthood Leaders' Comments and Suggestions

The priesthood leader section has two parts: first is the bishop's or branch president's recommendation, and second is the stake president's recommendation. Though this section is second in the paperwork, it is generally not filled out until you have completed all the other sections. You will meet with your bishop and he will review all the papers and give you a worthiness interview. He will ask about your testimony of the restored gospel of Jesus Christ, and make sure you are worthy, willing, and able to serve a mission. He will write a few comments on your application about what he thinks of your leadership potential, interests, talents, or limitations that should be considered in determining your mission assignment. A similar interview and written assessment will then be done by your stake president, or mission president, if you live in an area where no stake is organized.

3. Education and Service of Missionary Candidate

You are asked in this section to list your native language and any other languages you speak or have studied, as well as your desire to learn a new language. You will describe your educational background, including seminary and institute attendance, work experience, and military service. Here you also specify any extracurricular activities, special skills, accomplishments, previous Church callings, and other leadership experience.

This is also the section where you will outline how you will be financing (i.e., paying for) your mission and any special circumstances you have. Describe your source of funds, indicating how much money will be contributed from yourself, your family, your ward or branch, and other sources. Explain any special circumstances that the General Authorities should consider when making your mission call. Special circumstances could be emotional issues, physical limitations, personality disorders, or other things that could influence your ability to serve.

4. Unit Information for Missionary Candidate

If you have the physical paperwork, a ward or branch leader (probably the clerk) will need to complete this section for you. This information includes: your membership record number, your home ward or branch unit number, the name of your bishop or branch president, and the name of your stake president. If you are using the online recommendation system, this data is already in the system.

5. Personal Health History of Missionary Candidate

Here you are asked to specify whether you have had about 50 different medical conditions, including: serious injuries, various diseases, allergies, seizures, asthma, diabetes, tattoos, skin conditions, severe headaches, insomnia, tumors, cancers, learning disabilities, emotional instability, been a victim of abuse, used illegal drugs, etc. Answer all of the questions completely and honestly as it will help the team of doctors and authorities at Church headquarters understand your circumstances and capacity to serve.

6. Physician's Health Evaluation

You will need to bring this section of the mission application form with you to the doctor's office. The doctor will write down your height, weight, and blood pressure. A urinalysis and various other tests will be completed: blood tests, a tuberculosis test, etc. The doctor will fill in your immunization dates (MMR, Polio, Hepatitis A and B), and give an overall missionary fitness report (the doctor's assessment of your ability to serve). The doctor will note any physical or medical limitations you have and may recommend whether or not you can serve in certain parts of the world. This part of the form is concluded with the physician's signature, name, address, and other contact information.

7. Dental Evaluation for Missionary Candidate

Every missionary candidate needs to have a complete oral examination and the corresponding form sections filled out by a dentist. All dental treatment, including active orthodontic treatment (braces), must be completed before a prospective missionary begins to serve. (Wearing a retainer is permissible and not considered active treatment.) Have your dental examination early, perhaps as early as 6 months before you plan to go on your mission, to allow plenty of time to complete all dental treatments or your application may be delayed. The dentist will need to certify that you will be free of dental problems during the next two years, assuming proper oral hygiene is practiced. For many missionaries this will mean having your wisdom teeth removed before going on a mission.

8. Personal Insurance Information of Missionary Candidate

The final section of the mission application form is several pages of authorizations, releases of information, and medical privacy notices that you and your parents will need to sign. Personal health insurance is not required for you to serve a mission, but if you have health insurance coverage, the Church asks that you please do not cancel it. You will need to provide information about your health insurance policy so the Church can properly process your medical expenses for events that may happen on your mission. If you become sick or injured during your mission, the Church will provide initial payment for medical expenses, but that is not intended to replace your personal insurance. Health care expenses paid by the Church on your mission are made from the general funds of the Church and are thus sacred in nature and should be treated as such. But remember, if you do not have health insurance, you do not need to purchase it just for your mission.

Mission Paperwork Complete

Throughout the process of filling out your mission application, stay in contact with your bishop or branch president. Let him know your progress and ask him about any questions you might have. Once the forms are complete, you will need to make an appointment with your bishop and after that with your stake president. You will give them the application to review, and ultimately your stake president is the one who submits it to Church headquarters in Salt Lake City.

Remember, by the time you are submitting your application, the paperwork may have changed and the process may be different than what I have discussed in this book. If you have further questions about the mission application paperwork, please consult with your local priesthood leaders.

Chapter 4   Timeline: When to Start/How Long to Expect

"We issue the call again for all spiritually, physically, and emotionally qualified young men to come forth prepared to become missionaries in the Church of Jesus Christ. Be certain that you easily clear the minimum standards for service as a missionary and that you are continually raising the bar. Prepare yourself to be more effective in this great calling" (L. Tom Perry, "Raising the Bar," October, 2007).

Now that you've gotten an overview of the application process and seen the details of the paperwork you'll be completing, I'd like to address another one of the major areas of concern for young people who are soon to go on a mission. Most young men and women preparing to submit their mission papers want to know when to start the application process. Below I will walk you through, in more detail, a recommended mission application timeline. These are the steps involved in the mission call process, when to begin each part, and roughly how long to expect each of the steps to take. Please note that the time frames are approximate; each step could be faster than the estimate, or it could take longer depending on your individual circumstances.

Set Your Availability Date

As you can see in Figure 2, the timing for when to start the application process depends on your availability date. The first step is to determine the date you are available to start serving a full-time mission. The availability date is generally the day you turn 19 if you're a young man, or the day you turn 21 for a young woman. Your availability date should not be prior to this birthday, but could be later depending on circumstances such as schooling. Consult with your parents and local Church leaders if you need help in determining your availability date.

Four Months Prior: Start Application Process

Roughly four months prior to your availability date, you should plan to begin the application process. As we've covered, starting your mission papers is done by setting up a meeting with your bishop. He will review the spiritual and physical requirements to serve a mission. He will tell you about the application process and how to get started. Your bishop will either give you the physical forms, or he will give you directions to log in to the online website for mission papers.

This is when you will want to go to the doctor and dentist to have them fill out the medical forms in the application. If you have known dental issues you may want to go to the dentist even earlier. This is also a good time to start taking the Church's temple preparation course. And if you haven't gotten your patriarchal blessing by this point, you'll want to make arrangements to do that as well.

MISSION APPLICATION TIMELINE

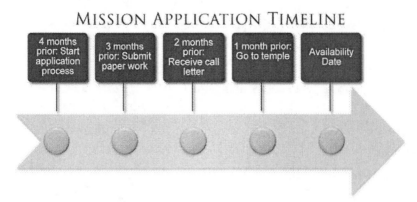

Figure 2: An approximate timeline for the mission application

Three Months Prior: Submit Paperwork

Approximately three months before your availability date you will want to have all the paperwork completed and ready for submission to Church headquarters. It generally takes at least a month to complete all the doctor and dentist visits, fill out the application, and meet with your bishop and stake president. The stake president, who ultimately submits your mission application to Church headquarters, is instructed not to send in the paperwork more than three months prior to your availability date. Although you don't have to submit it that early, it would be good to aim for that three month mark in case you are unexpectedly delayed in completing the paperwork.

Two Months Prior: Receive Mission Call Letter

After the application is submitted, depending on several factors, you should get your mission call letter in about two to four weeks. That letter will have your mission assignment and the date to report to the MTC. The Church normally tries to allow two to four months between the issuing of the call and the beginning of the mission. The packet you receive from Church headquarters will include additional instructions and information from your mission president specific to your mission. We'll discuss in detail the contents of the mission call packet in the next chapter.

One Month Prior: Go To the Temple

LDS temples are an integral part of missionary work and missionaries generally go to the holy temple to receive their endowment just prior to leaving on their mission. Through the temple endowment, missionaries receive knowledge, power, and protection from on high to do their work. The Church also has a seven-lesson temple preparation course that future missionaries are encouraged to attend. Talk to your bishop or other local Church leaders about arrangements for this class; you'll probably want to start taking the temple prep course around the same time you start your missionary application.

A Few Days Prior: Get Set Apart

Depending on the distance you have to travel to the Missionary Training Center (MTC), your stake president will set you apart as a full-time missionary a few days before your entrance into the MTC. After you've been set apart, you are an official missionary, and you will be expected to conduct yourself like one. If you live within driving distance to the MTC, your family will likely drive you there. If you live a long distance from the MTC, the Church headquarters will help you book a flight or make other travel arrangements. Once you enter the MTC your life will change forever. We'll talk more about the MTC later.

So that's it. Now you've seen the overview and we've reviewed the steps and the mission application timeline. Again, please note that the timeline estimates are approximate. Though the details of the application steps are accurate at the printing of this book, the Church may make alterations to the process in the future. So be sure to work with your bishop or branch president through every step of the process.

Missionaries Are Called by God

A great talk about the LDS Mission Call Process was given by Elder Ronald A. Rasband's in the April 2010 Priesthood Session of General Conference called *The Divine Call of a Missionary*. In the talk, Elder Rasband explains that missionaries are called by God through inspiration to living prophets. He also explains how the Apostle who makes the mission call uses the information from the missionary's application. I believe that understanding this part of the process will help you future missionaries know your call is truly from the Lord, and it will help you endure the sometimes lengthy and tedious application process.

"I joined Elder Eyring early one morning in a room where several large computer screens had been prepared for the session. There was also a staff member from the Missionary Department who had been assigned to assist us that day.

"First, we knelt together in prayer. I remember Elder Eyring using very sincere words, asking the Lord to bless him to know "perfectly" where the missionaries should be assigned. The word "perfectly" said much about the faith that Elder Eyring exhibited that day.

"As the process began, a picture of the missionary to be assigned would come up on one of the computer screens. As each picture appeared, to me it was as if the missionary were in the room with us. Elder Eyring would then greet the missionary with his kind and endearing voice: "Good morning, Elder Reier or Sister Yang. How are you today?"

"He told me that in his own mind he liked to think of where the missionaries would conclude their mission. This would aid him to know where they were to be assigned. Elder Eyring would then study the comments from the bishops and stake presidents, medical notes, and other issues relating to each missionary.

"He then referred to another screen which displayed areas and missions across the world. Finally, as he was prompted by the Spirit, he would assign the missionary to his or her field of labor.

"From others of the Twelve, I have learned that this general method is typical each week as Apostles of the Lord assign scores of missionaries to serve throughout the world.

"Having served as a missionary in my own country in the Eastern States Mission a number of years ago, I was deeply moved by this experience. Also, having served as a mission president, I was grateful for a further witness in my heart that the missionaries I had received in New York City were sent to me by revelation.

"… At the end of the meeting Elder Eyring bore his witness to me of the love of the Savior, which He has for each missionary assigned to go out into the world and preach the restored gospel. He said that it is by the great love of the Savior that His servants know where these wonderful young men and women, senior missionaries, and senior couple missionaries are to serve. I had a further witness that morning that every missionary called in this Church, and assigned or reassigned to a particular mission, is called by revelation from the Lord God Almighty through one of these, His servants."

My brothers and sisters who are preparing to go on a mission, I add my testimony that you will be called by God to go where the Lord needs you. There are people you need to meet and work with for their benefit and yours. I know it was the Lord's will for me to go to Rosario, Argentina, to teach and baptized the people I met there. So it will be for you.

When you submit your paperwork, you commit to go wherever the Lord wants you to go. May God bless and be with you as you prepare, as you submit your paperwork, and as you serve the Lord as one of his very special missionaries.

Chapter 5   The Mission Call Letter

"I remember fondly our entire family's great joy when two of our children received their calls to serve as full-time missionaries. Excitement and anticipation filled our hearts as they each opened their special letter from the prophet of God. Our daughter Jenessa was called to the Michigan Detroit Mission, and our son, Christian, was called to the Russia Moscow South Mission. What humbling and thrilling experiences, all at the same time" (Ronald A. Rasband, "The Divine Call of a Missionary," April 2010)!

A vital step in the LDS mission call process, and one that is the focus of much anticipation by the future missionary as well as for family and friends, is receiving the mission call letter. After you've filled out your mission papers and the application is submitted, it is a very anxious few weeks that you have to wait before finding out where you have been called to serve.

In due course, though, that envelope will arrive from Church headquarters. Some of you will choose to open the mission call packet in private, in your bedroom, or perhaps you'll get away to somewhere in nature. Many of you will gather around with your close family, and others will open the packet in the presence of a large number of family and friends. Many will even have a virtual gathering, over the phone or using online video conferencing, as you open your mission call letter. However you choose to do it, if you are spiritually prepared, opening and reading your mission call letter will bring many feelings: spiritual confirmations, excitement, and tears of joy.

Mission Call Packet

About two to four weeks after the Church receives your mission application, an envelope will arrive from The Church of Jesus Christ of Latter-day Saints Office of the First Presidency. The packet generally contains these items:

- The Call Letter from the Prophet
- A Letter from your Mission President
- A Letter from the MTC President
- General Instructions Checklist, including a list of clothing and other items to bring

The Call Letter from the Prophet

When you open your mission call packet, the first thing you will see will be the call letter from the prophet. It will be addressed to you and will say, "Dear Elder or Sister _____, You are hereby called to serve as a missionary of The Church of Jesus Christ of Latter-day Saints. You are assigned to labor in the _____ mission." This is the point where people tend to erupt into cheers and tears. Once you're able to continue, the letter will go on to tell you the language you will be speaking during your mission, and it will tell you where and when to report to the Missionary Training Center.

The letter will tell you your purpose as a missionary, "to invite others to come unto Christ by helping them receive the restored gospel through faith in Jesus Christ and His Atonement, repentance, baptism, receiving the gift of the Holy Ghost, and enduring to the end." In the letter, the prophet also will ask you to work to become an effective missionary, to remain worthy, and he will mention some of the blessings of faithful missionary service. Finally, the letter from the prophet asks you to send a written acceptance letter, and then it is signed by our living prophet, the president of the Church.

Letter from your Mission President

Another major piece of your mission call packet will be a welcome letter and orientation material from the mission president with whom you will be serving. He will express his testimony of mission work and his gratitude for your choice to serve a mission. He will express his joy and congratulations that you will be joining his mission and that you will be engaged together in the greatest cause in the entire world.

Your mission president will remind you that, as a missionary, you will become an ambassador of the Lord Jesus Christ. He will encourage you to continue reading the scriptures and preparing spiritually, including acquainting yourself with the Preach My Gospel manual.

He may tell you a little about the people and places of your mission and encourage you to learn to love the people where you will serve. He may also have mission-specific instructions, in addition to those general instructions you will receive from Church headquarters, such as clothing that may differ from the norm due to weather conditions in your mission.

Letter from the MTC President

In the mission call packet, you will also receive instructions and a congratulatory letter from the president of the MTC where you will be receiving your missionary training. He will also express his gratitude for your decision to serve the Lord, and his excitement about your arrival to the Missionary Training Center. He will advise you of medical issues that need to be addressed prior to your arrival, such as getting a seasonal flu shot. There will also be information such as your MTC mailing address and your assigned email address, which you will use throughout your mission. He may also provide contact phone numbers and website addresses where you can get more information.

There was once a time when most missionaries went to the MTC in Provo, Utah. But now there are over a dozen MTCs scattered across the world. If there is an MTC in the country where you have been called to serve, you very well could be assigned to that Missionary Training Center for part or all of your training time. The letter from your MTC President will discuss arrival times, transportation, and other information you will need to know about getting started on your mission.

General Instructions Checklist

The General Instructions Checklist will tell you the things you need to do right away, and the things you'll need to do before entering the MTC. It will advise you to complete any medical tests, treatments, and dental work before entering the MTC, including obtaining all required vaccinations outlined in the medical information section of the call packet.

This checklist will advise you to continue to prepare spiritually through prayer and scripture study, especially studying the Book of Mormon. It will instruct you to go to the temple to receive your endowment, and receive a patriarchal blessing, if you have not previously received them.

It will tell you to get a missionary haircut before arriving at the MTC and to be sure to show up in missionary attire. It will have a list of clothing, luggage, and other items you'll need to bring on your mission. We will review that list in more detail in Chapter 8.

Other Miscellaneous Items in the Call Packet

All together the packet can be a dozen or more pages depending on your mission and circumstances. There is frequently included a short biographical sketch of the mission president and his wife, an outline of behavior expected of missionaries, guidelines for getting ready for the mission, a section on missionary dress standards, medical requirements, a map of your mission, a short description of the area in which you will serve, and official Church contact information if you have further questions.

No matter where you are called to serve, remember that missionaries are called by God through prophecy and revelation to our living prophets and apostles. It is a great privilege to serve as an ambassador of our Lord and Savior Jesus Christ and to represent His true Church on the earth today. As a missionary, you will be an instrument in His hands to bring people into His fold for their eternal salvation. Getting your mission call letter means you are one step closer.

Section III. Temporal and Physical Preparation

Chapter 6   The LDS Mission Cost

"To you younger boys, may I encourage you to save money now for a future mission. Put it in a place where it is safe, not in a speculative account where it may be endangered. Consecrate it for this great purpose, and let it not be used for any other. Prepare yourselves. Attend seminary and institute. Prayerfully read the Book of Mormon. I hear much these days of costly youth excursions to exotic places during spring breaks and at other times. Why not stay near home and put the money in your future missionary accounts? Someday you will be grateful you did" (Gordon B. Hinckley, "The Question of a Mission," April 1986).

As you know, Mormon missionaries are expected to pay their own expenses while on their mission. This is a sacrifice and a privilege. This volunteer missionary force is the primary driver of the growth of the LDS Church throughout the world. Of course, for many missionaries and their families, the cost is an area of concern. In fact, one of the most frequent questions I get from readers of my website, MormonMissionPrep.com, is: how much does an LDS mission cost?

The current monthly cost for a mission, as of the publication of this book in 2011, for young men and young women from the United States is $400 a month. That comes out to a total of $7,200 for 18-month missions for sister missionaries, and $9,600 for young men who serve two-year missions.

For young people, nearly $10,000 seems like a lot of money, and it certainly will take time, effort, and discipline to save it up. But in other respects living off $10,000 for two years is actually quite a bargain. The Church is able to keep missions relatively affordable for two reasons. One reason is the many generous donations to support the Church's general Missionary Fund. The other reason is that mission costs are equalized, so missionaries going to an expensive place to live pay the same as missionaries going places that are inexpensive.

Many years ago, even before my time on a mission, each missionary paid his or her own actual living expenses. So a mission to Japan, for example, would have been much more expensive than a mission to South America. But in 1990, a new program was introduced to equalize the financial responsibility for each missionary by utilizing the Church Missionary Fund. Now, all young missionaries pay a flat monthly rate into that fund. Each missionary is then allocated from that fund what he or she needs for the expenses in their particular mission. This approach has reduced the burden on individual missionaries and their families who may have been assigned to work in more expensive areas of the world.

The figures above are for young men and young women from the United States, but mission costs will vary for senior couples and for young people outside the U.S. To find out the current cost of an LDS mission outside the United States, please talk to your bishop or another Church leader in your country. For senior missionaries, costs are not equalized like they are for the young people, so there is a degree of variation in the costs depending on the type of mission and location. In the United States, the average cost of a mission for couples who do not live at home is approximately $1,500 per month. Mission costs for senior missionaries can range, though, from $800 to $4,000 per month (which includes expenses for housing, utilities, food, and transportation), but about 80% of all senior missions cost less than $1,800 per month per couple.

Expenses Covered and Those Not Covered

Each young missionary throughout the world is given a monthly allowance designed to cover food, lodging, transportation, and other mission-related expenses. Some of the extra or optional expenses of mission, though, are not covered by this allowance. Missionaries are asked to bring extra personal money for non-essential additional items they would like to purchase such as souvenirs. And, of course, Church members around the world are asked to invite their local missionaries to have meals with them to help reduce the overall cost of the missionary program.

Start Saving for a Mission as Soon as Possible

Young people in the Church are encouraged to save money throughout their childhood and teenage years to pay for as much of their mission as they can. The blessings of missionary work are infinite and eternal, but there are costs and sacrifices that must be made. One of those sacrifices is the need for young men to save almost $10,000 to cover the costs of their mission. I have always believed that, as much as possible, young men should pay for their own missions because greater blessings flow that way.

This is what President Spencer W. Kimball said about paying for a mission in the May 1981 New Era magazine article called *President Kimball Speaks Out on Being a Missionary*:

"Remember it costs money to go to the various parts of the world and preach the gospel. Remember, then, it is your privilege now to begin to save your money. Every time money comes into your hands, through gifts or earnings, set at least part of it away in a savings account to be used for your mission.

"A young man's mission preparation consists of preparing to finance his mission so it may be his own contribution, so far as possible. How wonderful it would be if each future missionary could have saved for his mission from birth. How wonderful it would be if every boy could totally or largely finance his own mission and thereby receive most of the blessings coming from his missionary labors.

"Of course, if the boy is a convert in his teens, his years of saving are limited. If he lives in a country where the economic standards are low and opportunities are severely limited, he can still be governed by this policy so far as possible and do the best he can."

Tips on Saving Money for a Mission

Tip #1: Start early. It's never too early to start saving for your mission. When my son was four years old I got him a piggy bank to start saving for his mission. Starting early will help you develop better money management skills and habits, and it will also allow you to have interest work in your favor. Of course there are many young men who join the church in their late teenage years and are not able to start saving early. In those cases, do your best. Save all that you can and things will work out.

Tip #2: Find ways to earn money. Ask your parents, friends, and neighbors if they have chores you could do to earn money for your missionary fund. If you're ready and eager to work, you'll probably find your parents and friends are ready and eager to help you save money for your mission. And if you are disciplined in saving, you will find that the money from odd jobs will start adding up to something significant.

Here are some ideas for jobs to do for your parents or neighbors:

- Babysitting
- Collecting scrap metal to turn in for cash
- Delivering newspapers or having a paper route
- Dog walking or pet-sitting
- Gardening or pulling weeds
- Mowing grass or trimming lawns
- Putting newspapers by the front door for the elderly
- Raking leaves
- Shoveling snow from sidewalks and driveways
- Taking out the trash
- Tutoring (math, science, computers, etc.)
- Ask your parents about doing a yard sale or selling items online (could include things that you, your parents, or neighbors no longer need like clothes, toys, and electronic devices)

- Be creative. I once heard of a young man who did a magic show at birthday parties to earn extra money for his mission.

Tip #3: Budget! Make a budget, or plan, for how much of the money you earn will be saved for your mission. That budget should include, first and foremost, paying 10% of your earnings as tithing. You may want to allow yourself some money to spend on fun things, but you'll probably want to save as much as possible, hopefully at least 50% of each pay check, for your missionary fund.

Tip #4: Open a savings account. Talk to your parents about setting up a savings account. When you want to graduate from the piggy bank system, opening a savings account will be a safe way to store your money. This will also allow you to earn interest on the money you have saved.

Tip #5: Get a part-time job. When you get old enough, ask your parents about the possibility of getting a part-time job. They may let you get an after school job, or if your parents don't want you to work during the school year, ask them about getting a summer job. A part-time job will be a great way for you to add to your missionary fund. I got my first job working at a McDonald's restaurant when I was 16 years old. Within a couple of years, I was able to save about half of the money needed for my mission. Getting a job will teach you greater responsibility and give you further experience managing your money.

Tip #6: Talk to your parents. For many of these options, you will need your parents' help, so be sure to work with them to develop a plan for how to pay for your mission. Even if your parents can afford to pay for your mission, as President Kimball said, it is a good idea for young men and women to pay for some or all of their own mission expenses.

Supplemental Financial Assistance

If you alone are unable to meet the financial obligations of a mission, your parents, family, and friends may also contribute money on your behalf. Missionaries who have not saved the required funds may also obtain financial assistance from their home ward or stake, though the Church asks that you first get all the help you can from your family.

For many countries outside the U.S., if authorized, there is supplemental financial support available from the Church. If the missionary candidate cannot be supported fully from personal, family, ward or branch, or stake or district funds, then a request can be made for this financial assistance. Missionaries are asked not to request this special assistance until they, their family, their ward, and stake have committed themselves to provide all the financial support they can.

Source of Funds Section of Mission Papers

When filling out the mission application form, missionary candidates are asked to indicate the source of the funds, in other words, where the money will come from, in support of their mission. Be prepared to answer that question. Indicate on the form how much money will be contributed per month from: yourself, your family, your ward, and other sources.

Do all that you can to save for your mission. Start saving at an early age so that you can serve a faithful mission for the Lord and not be a financial burden on your family. The Lord will bless you many times over for the sacrifice of time and money you make to go on a mission.

And once you're on your mission, be sure to treat your monthly allowance of money carefully, for they are sacred funds. That money represents a sacrifice from you, your family, friends who may be contributing, and from people you don't even know who have donated to the Church's Missionary Fund.

Chapter 7   Skills for Living on Your Own

"An anxious mother of a prospective missionary once asked me what I would recommend her son learn before the arrival of his missionary call. I am certain she anticipated a profound response which would contain the more familiar requirements for service of which we are all aware. However, I said, 'Teach your son how to cook, but more particularly, teach him how to get along with others. He will be happier and more productive if he learns these two vital skills'" (Thomas S. Monson, "Who Honors God, God Honors," October 1995).

For many of you future missionaries, leaving on your mission will be the first time in your life that you have lived on your own, without mom and dad nearby. This chapter contains practical advice for missionaries, teenagers, and young adults who are preparing to live on their own. I'll review basic concepts concerning managing money, learning to cook, doing laundry, and time management. If you learn and use these skills, life on your mission will be much more pleasant.

Managing Money

When I arrived in my first assigned area in Argentina, in the city of Paraná, I was assigned to be companions with Elder Loesener who was a native Argentine from Buenos Aires. Elder Loesener, within the first couple of days, advised me to take $100 from my allowance and put it in an envelope in my suitcase to save in case of an emergency. That $100 was more than a third of my monthly allowance, but he assured me that we would make it through the month. He said we could pool our resources for buying food and any other needs. And though we scrimped that month, we still ate well and, after a few weeks of famous Argentine beef, I even put on a few pounds.

Getting through that first month was challenging, but from then on, I always had a $100 emergency reserve. If I ever ran out of money before the end of the month, I could tap into that reserve. Then in the next month, I tried to be more careful with my money and even save some to restock my emergency fund. This required careful management of my money, making a budget, and sticking to it. With that kind of fiscal discipline, I wasn't able to splurge, but I was able to have an occasional ice cream (a real treat for missionaries in Argentina).

Luckily, there weren't many major emergencies where I had to use my reserve, but there were times when our monthly allowance was late arriving. I was very glad, in times like that, to have some extra cash on hand to help get by. I heard many stories of missionaries running out of money half way through the month, but that never happened to me because I employed good money management skills.

Learning to Cook

In some areas of my mission, we ate at members' homes nearly every day. In other areas, I served in very small branches of the Church and the members rarely fed us. It was in those times that I was glad I knew how to cook. Making pancakes from scratch was not something I realized I'd be doing very often, but breakfast cereal was rare in Argentina, and the native breakfast beverage of "mate" (a type of tea) was off limits for missionaries.

Pasta, hamburgers, hot dogs, pizza, French toast, banana bread, soup, crepes, popcorn (on the stove top), and cookies were a few of the other things I whipped up from time to time during my mission. Future missionaries would do well to know how to cook a few of their favorite meals so they don't starve or have to survive on junk food, which would not provide the health, energy, and nutrition they need.

Perhaps this is also a good time to mention the need to learn to like a variety of foods. I was taught by my parents that missionaries should always be grateful for the meals given to them and that they should always eat what is in put in front of them. In Argentina, I was served just about every part of the cow imaginable. With only a few exceptions, like brain and tripe, I would at least give the food a try. Of course, we were also counseled by our mission president to avoid unhealthy or potentially dangerous foods, like Argentine blood sausage. Your mission president will advise you of things to avoid.

When I was new in my mission, it was still a little unclear to me what foods I needed to suffer through, and which were legitimately bad and should not be eaten. Once, in my first area, I found myself at the home of a member family for lunch. They served us "giso," a type of stew or soup, and as I put my spoon in the bowl, I noticed something strange floating around in it. Upon closer inspection, I realized those floating objects were little bugs in my soup! I didn't want to offend this humble, generous family. The bugs looked dead, and so I dutifully ate the whole bowl of giso. Had the bugs been alive, I don't think I could have done it. Luckily, the giso didn't make me sick, at least, no sicker than the water there, which we drank all the time.

Later in my mission, I learned that it was okay to turn down food that was legitimately bad or could make you sick. Almost wherever you go on your mission, there are diet and health issues to be aware of, so do be careful about what you eat.

But aside from bug-infested soup and the like, I think it's a good idea for missionaries to learn to be polite and eat the food that is so generously served to them. Future missionaries, start now to get used to eating a variety of foods. Perhaps ask your mom (or better yet, help your mom) to prepare meals from around the world to help you get your taste buds accustomed to new kinds of food.

Doing Laundry

Prior to my mission, I knew how to do laundry, or so I thought. I knew how to separate the lights from the darks, load the washing machine, put in soap, turn it on, and then switch the clothes to the dryer when it was complete. This is a great skill for any future missionary to learn because you'll most likely be doing your own laundry on your mission.

So while I thought I was prepared in this area, when I got to Argentina, I found no washing machines and no dryers in any of my apartments. In some of my areas, we were able to pay a woman in the ward to wash our clothes, but in as many as half of my areas, I had to wash my own clothes by hand. Needless to say, with me doing the laundry, it didn't take long for my white shirts to turn a shade of gray. Nevertheless they were clean, thanks to my trainer, Elder Loesener, who taught me the washboard method of doing laundry.

I'm not sure what the conditions are like in Argentina now, it's been more than ten years since I left. But it is likely that there, and in other parts of the world, missionaries are washing their own clothes by hand. So when you are learning to do laundry with the washing machine and dryer, you may also want to ask your mom for some tips on doing it by hand with a wash board, just in case.

Time Management

Though a mission seems like a long time, between 18 and 24 months, when you're older you will realize that it is really a very short time. Every moment on a mission counts and you must learn to make the best use of your time. Time management and planning will be key.

As a missionary you have daily and weekly times set aside in your schedule to plan for the coming days and week. You will carefully and prayerfully plan your meetings, lessons, meals, tracting, and other missionary activities so as to get the most out of each day.

You can start now to learn the secrets of time management through organizing and planning. As you get older, you will have more freedom and flexibility, and as you learn to handle your free time wisely, always making spiritual choices a priority, you will be guided by the Lord and become more responsible.

Here are some suggestions that will help you learn to make good decisions in managing your time.

- Make a calendar to schedule your activities of the week. On it, put set events such as school, sports practices or games, meals, chores, church meetings, etc.
- Make a weekly "to do" list of the most important tasks or activities that must be done such as homework assignments, chores, church activities, and other personal projects. Plan when you will do these between the set activities on your calendar.
- Review your "to do" list and calendar on a daily and/or weekly basis. Use your journal to keep track of major events and accomplishment.

The time on your mission is precious and must be used wisely in order to be an effective missionary. Managing your time well before your mission will also be key to your mission preparation effectiveness. Do not allow yourself to be sucked into mind-numbing activities for hours upon hours (like playing video games and listening to music) that often detract from the Spirit. Spend time learning to manage money, cook, do laundry, and other practical skills and you will be a more effective and happier missionary.

Chapter 8   What to Bring? Clothing List and Other Items

"To you missionaries that are about to go out, may I just suggest this to you: Make a commitment down in the bottom of your heart right now that you will never spend any day on your mission when you cannot honestly say to the Lord upon retiring, 'Today I did the very best I knew how.' I promise you in the name of the Lord Jesus Christ that if you can honestly say that, you do not need to worry about baptisms. You will not need to worry about success; you will have it." (M. Russell Ballard, "You—the Leaders in 1988," Ensign, Mar. 1979, 69–73)

As we discussed in chapter five about the mission call letter, your mission call packet will have a complete list of clothing and other gear you will need to bring with you on your mission. There are typical items that all missionaries need, which we will talk about below. Though slight variations do exist from one mission to another, for the most part, the clothing each missionary will need to bring is pretty standard. Your mission president will advise of any differences from the norm.

For more information on what to bring on your mission, you may want to check out the "what should I bring to the MTC" page on the Provo MTC website, http://www.mtc.byu.edu/miss-whattoknow.htm

Mission Gear and Clothing List

- Two bath towels and washcloths
- Twin-size bed sheets with a pillowcase
- A set of work clothes and gym clothes (jeans, t-shirt, shorts, athletic shoes, etc.)
- Cold-weather gear (gloves, hat, thermals, etc.) as needed
- Pajamas, robe, slippers, and other sleep-wear as needed
- A dark raincoat, lightweight plastic or nylon
- A pair of flip-flops and/or shower shoes
- An alarm clock (wind-up or battery)
- A backpack
- An umbrella
- A small first-aid kit
- A sewing kit
- Shaving equipment
- Deodorant and other toiletries

Gender-specific clothing is generally as follows:

Mission Clothing List: Elders	Mission Clothing List: Sisters
• 10 – 12 white shirts (some short sleeve and some long sleeve) • Two dark colored, conservative suits • 5 – 6 pair of dress slacks • 5 – 6 conservative ties • 8 – 10 solid, dark colored socks • Two pairs of thick-soled, comfortable, conservative shoes. • 8 – 10 pairs of temple garments • Waterproof winter boots, as needed • A dark overcoat with liner, as needed • Sweater(s), solid dark color, as needed	• 4 – 5 outfits of modest design: blouses, skirts, dresses, jackets, vests, jumpers, suits. Mid-calf length. Nothing tight-fitting or baggy; no wrap-around skirts, t-shirts, polo-shirts, denims, or leathers. • 12 pairs of nylons or knee-highs • 2 – 3 pairs of shoes that are conservative and comfortable • One pair of dress shoes • One pair of winter boots • 8 – 10 pairs of temple garments • Modest and durable underclothing • A dark winter coat • Sweater(s), as needed

If there are variations from the standard list of clothing and gear, then your mission president will advise you in his letter. Detailed standards for dress and grooming, including picture examples, will be sent in your mission call packet.

> You can find the latest guidelines for dress and appearance of missionaries at the Provo MTC website, http://mtc.byu.edu/miss-dressguidelines.htm

Missionary Luggage

Mormon missionaries are suggested to bring three pieces of luggage that follow these guidelines: Two large suitcases that you could check at the airport and one smaller bag (a carry-on). The first large suitcase should be no larger than 62 dimensional inches (height plus width plus depth), and no heavier than 70 pounds. The second piece should be no larger than 55 dimensional inches and no heavier than 70 pounds. The smaller, carry-on bag should be no larger than 45 dimensional inches.

The Approved Missionary Reading List

Mission rules state that missionaries are only to read from certain books and materials while they serve and that includes while in the MTC and in the field. Missionaries are not supposed to read newspapers or novels, for example, nor are they supposed to read from the many LDS-related Church books. There are, at times and under certain circumstances, exceptions to the approved reading list. Your mission president will advise you of any of those exceptions. In fact, some mission presidents may expressly ask you to read a book not on the list.

For the most part, though, the approved reading list is standard for all missionaries. The following is the Church-approved list of the reading material for missionaries. The list does change from time to time, but it is accurate as of the writing of this book (2011).

- The Scriptures and official Church study aids
- The Preach My Gospel Manual
- Official Church magazines (The Ensign, Liahona, etc.)
- Other Church lesson manuals and official Church materials
- The Church News
- Books in the Missionary Reference Library
  - o Jesus the Christ, by James E. Talmage
  - o Our Heritage: A Brief History of the Church of Jesus Christ of Latter-day Saints
  - o Our Search for Happiness, by M. Russell Ballard
  - o True to the Faith

The books of Missionary Reference Library are sold individually or together at the LDS Online Store, store.lds.org, and at Church Distribution Centers.

What NOT to Bring on Your Mission

Current Church guidelines are that missionaries are not to bring the following items to the MTC or to the mission field:

- Briefcases
- Any books not listed above
- Daily planners, including electronic planners
- Laptop or other computers
- Any video recording devices, or any video or DVD players
- Cellular phones, pagers, e-mail devices, or unauthorized electronic equipment
- Radios or clock radios
- Musical instruments
- Playing cards, games, balls, or any other kind of sports or hobby equipment
- Packages for other missionaries in the MTC or in the mission field
- Weapons of any kind

Conclusion: Temporal and Physical Preparation

That wraps up the section on temporal and physical preparation for your mission. We've talked about the cost of a mission, how to save money, advice on learning skills for living on your own, the mission call letter, and what to bring on your mission.

May the Lord bless you and be with you as you get yourself temporally and physically prepared for your mission. I hope the advice I have given is helpful, but if you have any further questions, please talk to your bishop or other local Church leaders.

We will next turn our attention to the spiritual aspects of mission preparation. As important and pressing as the temporal and physical aspects of mission prep are, it is the spiritual preparation that is most important. It is your spiritual preparation that will have the greatest impact on how effective you are as a missionary.

The mission call process, and other aspects of temporal and physical preparation for a mission, will change from time to time. Please check my website, www.MormonMissionPrep.com for the most up-to-date information.

Section IV. Becoming an Effective Missionary— Spiritual Prep

Chapter 9   Worthiness Requirements and Repentance Process

"If our thoughts remain clean and pure, we would never commit acts that would prevent us from serving in the mission field. All too common among young men today is the idea that they can sin a little, live it up with the boys, and then settle down for a short season before they are ready to be called so they can qualify themselves for missionary service. What fallacy there is in that philosophy" (L. Tom Perry, "Called to Serve," April 1991)!

I started the Mormon Mission Prep website to teach and inspire the next generation of missionaries. For whatever reason, from the beginning, I was frequently asked questions about worthiness qualifications for missionary service. Though I didn't seek these types of questions, I do want to help young people meet the worthiness standards of being a representative of the Lord. Therefore, in this section, we will discuss in detail what it means to be worthy to serve a mission, with particular emphasis on the law of chastity and the repentance process.

In no way do I wish to replace the divinely appointed role of parents and priesthood leaders. Your parents and local leaders want you to meet the standards for missionary service. They should be the first people you go to if you have questions about your worthiness. Your bishop has priesthood authority and spiritual gifts of discernment and judgment. Feel confident that he will gently and lovingly guide you through the process of qualifying in every way to be a full-time missionary.

The prophets of the Lord have long taught that every worthy young man should serve a mission and that every young man should strive to keep himself worthy. You cannot be a powerful missionary unless you have the Spirit of the Lord, and you cannot have the Spirit unless you have been cleansed of sin.

One of the more frequent questions I've received from young people regarding worthiness is law of chastity violations and the ability to later go on a mission. Many young people who have had issues with sexual morality want to repent and go on a mission. Frequently, though, young people in these circumstances do not know if their prior actions will prohibit them from ever serving.

While it is far better to never engage in these transgressions, let me reassure you that they can be repented of, and many times these young people can eventually go on a mission. Law of chastity issues are very serious in the sight of the Lord, though, and if serious enough, or if not fully repented of, they may disqualify you from going on a mission.

What is the Law of Chastity?

The law of chastity is the Lord's commandment that we keep ourselves sexually pure. For young people preparing for a mission, sexual purity means refraining from sexual relations and other sexual perversions such as homosexual activity, masturbation, viewing pornography, and petting (inappropriate touching). Here is a concise definition of chastity from the LDS True to the Faith manual:

> Chastity is sexual purity. Those who are chaste are morally clean in their thoughts, words, and actions. Chastity means not having any sexual relations before marriage. ...In the world today, Satan has led many people to believe that sexual intimacy outside of marriage is acceptable. But in God's sight, it is a serious sin. It is an abuse of the power He has given us to create life. The prophet Alma taught that sexual sins are more serious than any other sins except murder and denying the Holy Ghost (see Alma 39:3–5).

Sometimes people try to convince themselves that sexual relations outside of marriage are acceptable if the participants love one another. This is not true. Breaking the law of chastity and encouraging someone else to do so is not an expression of love. People who love each other will never endanger one another's happiness and safety in exchange for temporary personal pleasure.

Our Heavenly Father has given us the law of chastity for our protection...Those who keep themselves sexually pure will avoid the spiritual and emotional damage that always comes from sharing physical intimacies with someone outside of marriage.

Priesthood Leaders Determine Worthiness

As much as I want to and try to help young people who contact me about law of chastity concerns, these issues must be worked through with priesthood leaders before a potential missionary can be declared worthy to serve. Elder M. Russell Ballard, in a talk called *The Greatest Generation of Missionaries* (Ensign, November 2002) said, "as divinely appointed judges in Israel, the bishop and the stake president determine worthiness and resolve concerns on behalf of the Church." If you are struggling with sexual sin, please, talk to your parents and make an appointment to go see your bishop or branch president. They will love and support you and help you through the repentance process.

In that same talk, Elder Ballard went on to say,

"Please understand this: the bar that is the standard for missionary service is being raised. The day of the 'repent and go' missionary is over. You know what I'm talking about, don't you, my young brothers? Some young men have the mistaken idea that they can be involved in sinful behavior and then repent when they're 18 1/2 so they can go on their mission at 19. While it is true that you can repent of sins, you may or you may not qualify to serve. It is far better to keep yourselves clean and pure and valiant."

Raising the Bar

President Gordon B. Hinckley also spoke of the need to raise the worthiness standards for missionaries. In fact, he commented on Elder Ballard's talk saying:

"Elder Ballard has spoken to you concerning missionaries. I wish to endorse what he said. I hope that our young men, and our young women, will rise to the challenge he has set forth. We must raise the bar on the worthiness and qualifications of those who go into the world as ambassadors of the Lord Jesus Christ" ("To Men of the Priesthood," Ensign, Nov. 2002, 57).

President Hinckley further said:

"The time has come when we must raise the standards of those who are called ... as ambassadors of the Lord Jesus Christ. ... We simply cannot permit those who have not qualified themselves as to worthiness to go into the world to speak the glad tidings of the gospel" ("Missionary Service," Worldwide Leadership Training Meeting, Jan. 11, 2003, 17).

Elder L. Tom Perry has also spoken on missionary worthiness, comparing these standards with those needed to enter the house of the Lord, the holy temple. Said he, "Personal worthiness is the minimum spiritual standard for serving a mission. This means that you are worthy in every way to make and to keep sacred temple covenants" (Raising the Bar, Ensign, November 2007).

Worthiness Interview

As I mentioned above, only a bishop (or branch president) can interview missionary candidates and recommend them as worthy to serve a full-time mission. In this interview, your priesthood leader will ask you if you meet the qualifications for missionary service revealed in section four of the Doctrine and Covenants: Faith, hope, charity, love, an eye single to the glory of God, virtue, knowledge, temperance, patience, brotherly kindness, godliness, charity, humility, and diligence.

Full-time missionary service is a privilege, not a right. Therefore, potential missionaries must be worthy in every respect in order to receive that privilege. If you have had law of chastity violations, or been involved in other serious sins, your bishop and stake president will need to confirm that your repentance is complete prior to submitting your mission application. They will make sure that you are prepared spiritually for your mission call and that you have been free of transgression for a sufficient time to manifest genuine repentance. If you have had multiple or serious violations of the law of chastity, this time period will likely be at least one year from the most recent occurrence.

The Repentance Process

Whether you have committed major sins or not, to prepare for a mission, all young people will need to become worthy and utilize the repentance process. Many youth, especially those who have committed serious sins that require confession to the bishop, are a little afraid or unsure how to begin the repentance process. Let's review the divinely revealed steps.

- *Faith in God.* Repentance is an act of faith in Jesus Christ, and doing so acknowledges the power of His Atonement. It is only through the grace of our Lord and Savior that we can be forgiven, and we therefore must adhere to the terms He has set forth. As we recognize the power of the Atonement to cleanse us from sin, we "exercise [our] faith unto repentance" (Alma 34:17).
- *Sorrow for Sin.* Sincere repentance means acknowledging that we have sinned against God's commandments. This admission will lead to "godly sorrow," which "worketh repentance to salvation" (2 Corinthians 7:10). Godly sorrow will naturally lead you to a sincere desire to change and a willingness to complete the requirements for forgiveness.
- *Confession.* "Whoso confesseth and forsaketh [sin] shall have mercy" (Proverbs 28:13). Repentance means going before God in humble prayer, acknowledging your sins, and pleading for His help. Serious transgressions, such as violations of the law of chastity, also need to be confessed to the Lord's priesthood representatives who are your local bishop or branch president. While only the Lord can forgive sins, these leaders play a divine role and will help you through the repentance process.

- *Abandonment of Sin.* The Lord has said, "By this ye may know if a man repenteth of his sins—behold, he will confess them and forsake them" (D&C 58:43). To forsake means to abandon, renounce, or give up. True repentance means resolving that we will forsake our sins and never repeat the transgression.
- *Restitution.* Another part of repentance is restoring, as far as possible, all that has been damaged by our sinful actions. Whether that means fixing someone's property or someone's reputation, restitution shows the Lord that we are doing all we can to repent and change our ways.
- *Righteous Living.* Repentance is not complete until we fill our lives with good choices and endure to the end in righteousness. We must engage in activities that bring spiritual power like reading the scriptures and praying daily for the Lord to give us strength beyond our own.

My young brothers and sisters, the Lord loves you. If you have fallen into transgression, He has provided a way back. The road of repentance is available thanks to the Atonement of Jesus Christ. The Lord, your family, and Church leaders will help you repent and fully prepare for your mission.

For those of you striving and succeeding at keeping yourself clean and pure in spite of this increasingly sin-filled world in which we live, I applaud your faith and courage. If you always obey the Lord's commandments, especially the law of chastity as we have discussed, you will be spared the hardships that inevitably come when you violate God's commandments. You will keep yourself worthy to become one of the Lord's chosen representatives, and you will have immense joy and eternal blessings for the missionary work you will perform.

Missionary Work Helps Us Be Cleansed of Sin

Can I tell you one other little known fact about missionary work and worthiness? One of the blessings of missionary work is that it can help cleanse us from sin. Our Lord and Savior Jesus Christ has the power to cleanse us of sin, which power He possesses thanks to His suffering for the sins of the world. By faithfully doing missionary work, we do many of the things that are necessary to take advantage of the Atonement of Jesus Christ and become more clean and worthy.

When I arrived in Argentina and had a first interview with my mission president, he shared this scriptural concept and it has always stuck with me. The following are scriptural examples I have found that discuss how missionary work helps to cleanse us from sin:

- To early Church missionaries the Lord said, "And in this place let them lift up their voice and declare my word with loud voices, without wrath or doubting, lifting up holy hands upon them. For I am able to make you holy, and your sins are forgiven you." D&C 60:7
- To another group of early missionaries of the Church, the Lord said: "For I will forgive you of your sins with this commandment—that you remain steadfast in your minds in solemnity and the spirit of prayer, in bearing testimony to all the world of those things which are communicated unto you." D&C 84:61
- Praying about the 12 disciples He chose in the ancient Americas, our Savior said, "Father, I thank thee that thou hast purified those whom I have chosen, because of their faith, and I pray for them, and also for them who shall believe on their words, that they may be purified in me, through faith on their words, even as they are purified in me." 3 Ne. 19: 28
- When the Jaredites rejected the prophet Ether after he was sent to exhort them to believe in God, the Lord said, "If they have not charity it mattereth not unto thee, thou hast been faithful; wherefore, thy garments shall be made clean. And because thou hast seen thy weakness thou shalt be made strong, even unto the sitting down in the place which I have prepared in the mansions of my Father." Ether 12:37

Through scripture study, and from experience, I have found that sincere, true missionary efforts naturally lead to forgiveness of sins. By being a worthy missionary and helping others come unto Christ, we ourselves are brought closer to Him and receive His cleansing power. President Spencer W. Kimball stated: "The Lord has told us that our sins will be forgiven more readily as we bring souls unto Christ and remain steadfast in bearing testimony to the world, and surely every one of us is looking for additional help in being forgiven of our sins" (Ensign, Oct. 1977, p. 5).

It's not that doing missionary work gives you a free pass from your sins. It's that doing missionary work requires the individual to go through the God-given steps of faith, repentance, and cleansing ordinances of salvation, which make us worthy and able to return to live with God.

The main purpose of missionary work is to help bring others to Christ, but an important secondary purpose is that it brings the missionaries themselves closer to Christ. I thank Heavenly Father for this wonderful blessing of missionary work with its dual effects: gathering people of the world into Christ's fold, and purifying the missionary workers themselves.

Conclusion

Keeping yourself worthy is vital to mission preparation. When you keep yourself worthy, and honor the baptismal covenants (and priesthood covenants of the young men) you have made, you will have the Spirit of the Lord with you. The Holy Ghost will guide you in your missionary preparation, and he will guide you in your work as a missionary. You need the Spirit to teach and testify to the hearts and souls of those you meet. As you keep yourself worthy, you will have the Spirit with you and you will be a more effective instrument in the hands of the Lord.

Chapter 10   Using the Scriptures, Especially the Book of
Mormon: Another Testament of Jesus Christ

*"I have a vision of thousands of missionaries going into the
mission field with hundreds of passages memorized from the Book
of Mormon so that they might feed the needs of a spiritually
famished world. I have a vision of the whole Church getting nearer
to God by abiding by the precepts of the Book of Mormon. Indeed, I
have a vision of flooding the earth with the Book of Mormon."
(Ezra Taft Benson, "Flooding the Earth with the Book of
Mormon," November, 1988)*

The Book of Mormon plays an important role in missionary work
because when people read it with a sincere heart, the Spirit will testify
to their hearts that it is true (see Moroni 10: 3-5). When people know
the Book of Mormon is true, they will know that Joseph Smith was a
true prophet. And when they know that, they'll also know The Church
of Jesus Christ of Latter-day Saints is the only "true and living church"
upon the face of the earth today (see D&C 1: 30).

When I was in the MTC, I remember being taught how important
the Book of Mormon is in doing missionary work. I remember at that
time sincerely seeking to know why the Book of Mormon was so vital
to the work. I never doubted the book's truthfulness, but for a time I
wondered why the Lord would go to so much trouble to have the
Nephite prophets preserve the record, and for Joseph Smith to translate
it. I pondered and prayed about the subject for many days.

Then, I got a letter from my dad in which he bore powerful
testimony of the truthfulness of the Book of Mormon. He explained

how it had been the instrument in converting many, many souls that he personally knew. It was then that the Holy Spirit taught me that the Lord, if He wanted, could have chosen a different book or a different way to establish his word in the latter-days. But the Lord chose the Book of Mormon to be that instrument. And because the Lord prepared it, if we use it in our teaching, no other instrument brings the spirit more powerfully than the Book of Mormon in testifying of the truthfulness of our message.

This is what the Preach My Gospel manual says about the role of the Book of Mormon in missionary work:

The Book of Mormon is powerful evidence of the divinity of Christ. It is also proof of the Restoration through the Prophet Joseph Smith. An essential part of conversion is receiving a witness from the Holy Ghost that the Book of Mormon is true. As a missionary, you must first have a personal testimony that the Book of Mormon is true. This testimony can lead to a deep and abiding faith in the power of the Book of Mormon during the conversion process. Have confidence that the Holy Ghost will testify to anyone who reads and ponders the Book of Mormon and asks God if it is true with a sincere heart, real intent, and faith in Christ. This witness of the Holy Ghost should be a central focus of your teaching.

...The Book of Mormon, combined with the Spirit, is your most powerful resource in conversion. It is the most correct of any book on the earth (see introduction to the Book of Mormon). It teaches the doctrine of Christ plainly, especially in the lessons you teach investigators. Use it as your main source for teaching the restored gospel.

...A central purpose of the Book of Mormon is to convince all people that Jesus is the Christ (see title page of the Book of Mormon). It testifies of Christ by affirming the reality of His life, mission, and power. It teaches true doctrine concerning the Atonement—the foundation for the plan of salvation. Several of those whose writings are preserved in the Book of Mormon saw Christ personally. The brother of Jared, Nephi, and Jacob saw the premortal Christ. Mormon and Moroni saw the risen Christ. In addition, multitudes were present during the Savior's brief but powerful ministry among the Nephites (see 3 Nephi 11–28). Those who know little or nothing about the Savior will come to know

Him by reading, pondering, and praying about the Book of Mormon.

The Power of the Book of Mormon

The second area I served in during my mission was called the Rural Ward in the city of Santa Fe, Argentina. I had an experience there that I will always remember that taught me the power of the Book of Mormon. One day we had an appointment to teach a first discussion to a man named Eduardo and his family. We were doing exchanges with the zone leaders that day. My companion, Elder Maynes, went with one zone leader while the other one, Elder Rindlisbacher, came with me to the appointment with Eduardo.

We arrived at the appointment and sat down with the family in an outdoor terrace area. To our surprise, we found that the family had invited a friend to the appointment. This friend turned out to be their preacher, and he had come ready for a verbal sparring match ('Bible bash' as we often called it). Initially, the preacher sat back and listened as we began teaching the first principles of the first discussion (God the Father, Jesus Christ our Savior, Prophets, etc.). But soon the preacher began to ask contentious questions in an attempt to stump us, and before long he was lecturing to us, and we could hardly get a word in.

After listening patiently for 15 minutes or so, I finally decided to reach into my bag and pull out the Book of Mormon and read some passages from it. I did this in an attempt to testify of the truthfulness of our teachings, more than to directly answer his questions. To my surprise, at the very moment I pulled the Book of Mormon out of my bag, the preacher became quiet. I suddenly found myself with a captive audience, so I read a verse or two of scripture from the Book of Mormon. I testified that the book was of God, that it taught of Christ, and that it is a testament to the truthfulness of the LDS Church.

After that day, unfortunately, we never taught Eduardo or his family again. Yet I will never forget that moment, nor the power of the Book of Mormon displayed that day, to touch hearts through the Holy Ghost and silence opposing forces.

President Ezra Taft Benson once said:

"We are to use the Book of Mormon in handling objections to the Church... All objections, whether they be on abortion, plural marriage, seventh-day worship, etc., basically hinge on whether Joseph Smith and his successors were and are prophets of God receiving divine revelation. Therefore, the only problem the objector has to resolve for himself is whether the Book of Mormon is true. For if the Book of Mormon is true, then Jesus is the Christ, Joseph Smith was his prophet, The Church of Jesus Christ of Latter-day Saints is true, and it is being led today by a prophet receiving revelation" (A Witness and a Warning, 4–5).

The baptism of Augustín Zapata is a story that illustrates the power of the Book of Mormon in the conversion process.

I met Augustín Zapata after he had a first discussion with other missionaries. I had just been transferred to a new area, a city called Fray Luis Beltran. The previous Elders had found Augustín and had given him a Book of Mormon. When my companion and I returned to check up on Augustín a few days after the first discussion, we found that he had read the entire Book of Mormon. He loved the Book of Mormon and couldn't help but read it in its entirety and then start reading it again.

When I heard that, I thought Augustín was "golden" and that he would be baptized in short order. And while the Book of Mormon was a key to his conversion, it didn't quite turn out so simple.

We taught Augustín all the discussions. He greatly enjoyed our visits, he felt the Spirit while we were there, and he seemed believed everything that we taught him. But when we invited him to get baptized, he said he wasn't sure he could do that. His deceased father was a devout Catholic, and Augustín was afraid that he would offend his father if he joined another faith. I was unsure how to address his concern, so we encouraged him to continue praying and to come to Church with us to see how he liked the meetings and the people there.

Augustín agreed to come to Church, but week after week, he never showed up. Eventually, we offered to give him a ride to Church. We offered to stop by his house, walk with him to the bus, and even pay his fare. Still, week after week, when we showed up at his house, he would come up with excuses not to come to Church.

Finally, one Saturday night he promised us that he would come to Church the next morning. When we got to his house, though, once again Augustín said he couldn't come to Church. This made me angry. I shared my disappointment with Augustín and I walked away, vowing to myself to never visit him again.

A few weeks went by and we hadn't seen or heard from Augustín. Then one day, he saw us in the street and stopped us. Augustín said he had a dream, and his father came to him in this dream and told him to find the truth. Augustín said he thought the truth his father was referring to might be the Mormon Church. I then challenged Augustín to come to Church the following Sunday. I didn't offer to give Augustín a ride, thinking this would be a good test to see how sincere he was.

To my overwhelming joy, Augustín did come to Church, and he loved it. We sat in sacrament meeting together and Augustín picked up a hymn book and began singing along with the rest of the congregation. In Sunday School class, Augustín actively participated. During and after the meetings, he thoroughly enjoyed socializing with the other members. He felt the same spirit at our Church meetings as he had felt when reading the Book of Mormon, and he knew the way to keep that feeling was to get baptized and join the Church.

Augustín was baptized a few weeks later on the 24th of November, 1996, and it was a beautiful occasion. I know that it was the converting power of the Book of Mormon, as well as the Spirit he felt during the Church meetings, that helped Augustín Zapata make that decision to follow the Savior and join His true Church through baptism.

I know that the Book of Mormon is true. I have read it, I have prayed about it, and I have received a witness from God that it contains the words of our Savior Jesus Christ. It is perhaps the most powerful tool missionaries have because it brings the Spirit, which then teaches,

Figure 3: Elder Neil Adams, Augustin Zapata, and Elder Jimmy Smith at a church building near the city of Fray Luis Beltran, Argentina.

testifies, and converts hearts and minds. You will be a more powerful missionary by studying the Book of Mormon and knowing it well enough to use it frequently in your teaching. I encourage you future missionaries to read and gain a personal testimony of the Book of Mormon. By so doing, you will be a more prepared missionary, and thus a better instrument in the hands of the Lord.

The Bible

The Bible, the Old Testament and the New Testament, is another major part of Latter-day Saint scripture and an extremely valuable tool in missionary work. It provides a common foundation between LDS teachings and other Christians that believe the Bible to be the word of God. By reading the Bible, future missionaries can come to understand its doctrines and history, and gain a testimony of the gospel of Jesus Christ that is taught within its pages.

I feel for the Bible in a similar way as expressed by Abraham Lincoln when he said: "This Great Book ... is the best gift God has given to man. All the good the Saviour gave to the world was communicated through this book. But for it we could not know right from wrong" (Speeches and Writings, 1859–1865 [1989], 628).

I also echo the words of the Lord's apostle, Elder Jeffrey R. Holland, when he said, "We love and revere the Bible...The Bible is the word of God. It is always identified first in our canon, our 'standard works'" ("My Words . . . Never Cease", General Conference, April 2008).

Reading the Bible

One accomplishment I am very proud of is that I have read the Bible from cover to cover. It was a feat that took me about 15 years. I had read many parts of the Bible throughout my youth, in seminary and in family scripture study. On my mission, when I was in the MTC, I decided that I should read the Bible in its entirety. I started with the New Testament, and actually finished that before I left the MTC.

Then, when I got to the mission field, I started on the Old Testament. I think, by the end of my mission, I had only gotten through the first five books of Moses. When I got home from the mission, I neglected to continue reading it, favoring instead the reading of the Book of Mormon and other scriptures. After graduating from BYU, I picked up where I left off, and got over half way through the Bible. But once again, I got side tracked due to life and circumstances.

When I began working for the LDS Church a few years ago, I decided that I better finish my quest. I was riding the bus to and from work each day and this gave me time to get through the remainder of the Bible. It was not easy to read. There were many chapters that I didn't understand and were tough to get through. But I am grateful that I did it. I know the Bible is the word of God, and I can say that now with more power than ever before, having actually read every word in it.

When the 12th President of the Church, Spencer W. Kimball, was a young 14-year-old boy, he read the Bible from cover to cover and was forever grateful that he completed that goal. Here is what he said:

"Let me tell you of one of the goals that I made when I was still but a lad. When I heard a Church leader from Salt Lake City tell us at conference that we should read the scriptures, and I recognized that I had never read the Bible, that very night at the conclusion of that very sermon I walked to my home a block away and climbed up in my little attic room in the top of the house and lighted a little coal-oil lamp that was on the little table, and I read the first chapters of Genesis. A year later I closed the Bible, having read every chapter in that big and glorious book.

"I found that this Bible that I was reading had in it 66 books, and then I was nearly dissuaded when I found that it had in it 1,189 chapters, and then I also found that it had 1,519 pages. It was formidable, but I knew if others did it that I could do it.

"I found that there were certain parts that were hard for a 14-year-old boy to understand. There were some pages that were not especially interesting to me, but when I had read the 66 books and 1,189 chapters and 1,519 pages, I had a glowing satisfaction that I had made a goal and that I had achieved it.

"Now I am not telling you this story to boast; I am merely using this as an example to say that if I could do it by coal-oil light, you can do it by electric light. I have always been glad I read the Bible from cover to cover" (in Ensign, May 1974, 88).

The Holy Bible is a Miracle

Just like it is important for every missionary to gain his or her own testimony of the Book of Mormon, every current and future Mormon missionary should read and study the Bible and gain his or her own witness of its truthfulness. It teaches of Jesus Christ and how to live in a manner worthy to return to our Heavenly home. A deeper knowledge of the Bible will help missionaries and members alike come unto Jesus Christ. Elder M. Russell Ballard, a member of the Quorum of the Twelve Apostles, has said:

"The Holy Bible is a miracle! It is a miracle that the Bible's 4,000 years of sacred and secular history were recorded and preserved by the prophets, apostles, and inspired churchmen. It is a miracle that we have the Bible's powerful doctrine, principles, poetry, and stories. But most of all, it is a wonderful miracle that we have the account of the life, ministry, and words of Jesus, which was protected through the Dark Ages and through the conflicts of countless generations so that we may have it today. It is a miracle that the Bible literally contains within its pages the converting, healing Spirit of Christ, which has turned men's hearts for centuries, leading them to pray, to choose right paths, and to search to find their Savior."

"...My brothers and sisters, we must help all people, including our own members, understand the power and importance of the Holy Bible. The Bible is scripture that leads us and all mankind to accept Jesus Christ as our Savior. May God grant us the desire and capacity to accept and live His teachings" (The Miracle of the Holy Bible, General Conference, April 2007).

My young brothers and sisters, I cannot stress enough the importance of becoming familiar with the scriptures prior to your mission. Read from the scriptures daily, even if it is only a few verses. You will learn the doctrines of the gospel of Jesus Christ, and you will build your own testimonies. Perhaps at no point in your life will you have more ample time and reason to study the scriptures than on your mission. Take advantage of that time, read and study, ponder and pray about the Bible, the Book of Mormon, and the other standard works.

Scripture Mastery

One more thing I'd like to mention about using the scriptures is LDS Seminary Scripture Mastery. For those of you in high school and enrolled in Seminary, you know that studying the scriptures is a vital part of that program. The Scripture Mastery verses will help you (no surprise here) master the scriptures. If you do your Scripture Mastery faithfully for your four years in seminary, you will come away having memorized 100 very powerful scriptures.

Having the words of the scriptures, the "words of life," (see D&C 84: 85) at the top of your mind will make you a better-prepared missionary. Missionaries who know and use the scriptures will teach more powerfully, will be more likely to have the companionship of the Holy Ghost, and will be more effective in bringing souls unto Christ.

Chapter 11   The Missionary Training Center (MTC)

"My earnest hope for each of you young men is that you will not simply go on a mission—but that you will become missionaries long before you submit your mission papers, long before you receive a call to serve, long before you are set apart by your stake president, and long before you enter the MTC...You will not suddenly or magically be transformed into a prepared and obedient missionary on the day you walk through the front door of the Missionary Training Center. What you have become in the days and months and years prior to your missionary service is what you will be in the MTC" (David A. Bednar, "Becoming a Missionary," October 2005).

When my youngest brother Michael was going to the Missionary Training Center (MTC) in Provo, Utah, it had been 15 years since I had entered the MTC as a young missionary. In talking with him in the days before he entered, I realized he didn't know what to expect once he arrived there. So we, my brothers and I, did a special family home evening lesson where we gave him advice about what to expect at the MTC.

The MTC is where missionaries for The Church of Jesus Christ of Latter-day Saints get doctrinal and language training at the beginning of their missionary service. There are more than a dozen MTCs located in nations throughout the world, including Brazil, Japan, Mexico, and the United Kingdom. The flagship MTC is located in Provo, Utah, USA, adjacent to the campus of Brigham Young University. Missionaries who are not learning a language usually spend 3 weeks in the MTC, while those learning a foreign language will generally spend

73

9 to 12 weeks there. The MTC is a crucial part of getting missionaries prepared to serve, but it was not always so.

History of the MTC

In the early 1900s, new missionaries would report to the Mission Home in Salt Lake City, a small building adjacent to Temple Square. Missionaries would stay there just a day or two before leaving to their assigned areas. In November 1961, missionaries started heading a few miles south, to Brigham Young University, at the beginning of their mission for some language training. Soon, a new LDS mission, the Language Training Mission (LTM), was created, with the geographic boarders being the perimeter of the buildings, dormitories, and classrooms for the missionaries in training.

As the Church and the number of missionaries continued to grow, the missionary training program grew as well. The name of the LTM was changed to the Missionary Training Center in 1978, to note that it was for more than just language training. In 1998, all North American missionaries called to Brazil were sent to the Brazil MTC in São Paulo for the second month of their training. This was part of an integrated MTC program, originally thought of as a solution to overcrowding at the MTC in Provo. But it has also proven successful in better training missionaries and has revolutionized the MTC experience.

Your mission call packet will tell you the location of the MTC that will be giving you your missionary training and to which you will report on the first day of your mission. As I mentioned in Chapter 5, the call packet will also contain a letter from the president of the MTC and will inform you of MTC arrival times, transportation, and other information you will need to know about getting started on your mission.

Life at the MTC

Life inside the MTC is definitely different than life outside, but it is great. There's so much to learn in just a few weeks at the MTC:

- Gospel doctrines
- How to develop Christ-like attributes
- How to teach by the Spirit
- Communication skills
- A foreign language (for some)
- The mission rules, etc.

In the MTC, you will be assigned a companion and you will be part of a district of three or four other companionships. You will do all of your training classes and other activities with your companion and district and you will likely become great friends with them. Every day you will go to classes—classes about the gospel of Jesus Christ and classes on your language—with your district. Several times a week you will be able to go together to play sports or do other exercise in the gymnasium. Once a week you'll go to the temple, Sundays will be filled with Church meetings, and once a week you will have a devotional address by a General Authority. You'll have weekly service opportunities on the MTC campus ('celestial service,' as they called it). You will be taught by teachers who will help you grow and will affect your entire mission.

MTC Services

In a lot of ways, the MTC is a virtual city, providing you with all the services you need as a missionary. Here's a rundown of the services available at the Provo, Utah MTC:

- *Banking services*—An office at the MTC has capabilities to cash checks and also sells travelers' checks.

- *Barbershop*—Elders are entitled to one or two haircuts depending on their length of stay at the MTC. Sister missionaries are not offered haircuts, although a beautician is available at the MTC for paid appointments.

- *Bookstore*—The bookstore is stocked with learning materials, book bags, and everyday items such as toiletries, white shirts, snacks, and treats.

- *Cafeteria*—Three meals a day are served. If missionaries happen to have a scheduling conflict, they can pack a sack lunch instead of eating in the cafeteria.
- *Copy center*—Services such as copying, laminating, or binding are available there.
- *Dry cleaning*—Rates are reasonable. There is a trend for missionaries to gain weight while at the MTC, so suit alterations are also available for a fee.
- *Gym*—Missionaries can exercise 60 minutes a day while in the MTC. The Provo MTC has a large gymnasium with basketball and volleyball courts. There are also weight lifting machines and exercise classes offered.
- *Laundry*—Washers and dryers are available to use on your preparation day. Missionaries must purchase their own detergent from vending machines or the bookstore.
- *Mail*—Letters are delivered directly to the missionaries' mailboxes, and packages can be picked up at a nearby window. The MTC will not accept hand deliveries, so you must send packages through the post office or private carriers.
- *Medical services*—The BYU health center is adjacent to the Provo MTC and provides most medical services missionaries need. Immunizations are available, and doctors are on call for emergencies.
- *Sheets and pillowcases*—All bed linens are provided by the MTC. Missionaries can exchange soiled sheets for clean linens on a weekly basis.

Visit http://mtc.byu.edu for a Virtual Tour of the Provo, Utah MTC. Also see that site's MTC FAQs page to get answers to additions questions.

My MTC Experience

I entered the Provo, Utah MTC in October 1995 on my way to serving in Rosario, Argentina. I was in one of the first trial programs of Technology Aided Language Learning (TALL), which I believe is now part of most missionaries' curriculum. I loved the MTC from the very beginning; everyone was so nice, and the spiritual growth I experienced was phenomenal.

I was in the MTC just after I completed my first year of college at BYU, and all the facilities (beds, laundry, cafeteria, etc.) were similar to what I was used to in the BYU dorms. I was amazed at how they just threw us into Spanish, teaching us to pray and contact people in Spanish on our very first day. At the MTC, in a lot of ways, I felt I had a stress-free life. I had no worries about what was going on in the outside world; I just studied Spanish and the gospel and felt the Spirit of the Lord all day, every day.

Other missionaries I knew, though, had a harder time. Many missionaries have a hard time learning the language and many have a hard time being spiritually minded in the way that is required at the MTC. If you have largely ignored spiritual matters throughout your life, then going to the MTC can be a difficult transition. This gives you even more reason to spiritually prepare before your mission.

Once you arrive at the MTC, your spiritual preparation will be accelerated. One faith-promoting experience I had was after I had been in the MTC for about a month. We had a lesson on faith, and as I sat there listening, my mind and soul seemed to open up and receive knowledge from heaven. After the class, one of the other missionaries asked me what I had learned about faith. As I began to convey through words what I had felt, the Spirit of the Lord poured over me like never before. The other missionaries and I were both greatly edified by this experience.

The more I learned about the restored gospel of Jesus Christ, the more I realized how much I didn't know. The more I studied the scriptures, the more I wanted to immerse myself in them and learn all that I could. The hour a day of personal scripture study they allot you at the MTC suddenly didn't seem like nearly enough.

I came away from the MTC with more gratitude in my heart, more meekness and penitence, and a stronger testimony of the Book of Mormon. I left the MTC with greater understanding of the importance of obedience to the commandments and to the mission rules. I had deeper gospel knowledge, a stronger testimony of the Church and of the atonement of Jesus Christ. I came away from the MTC with greater sensitivity to the Spirit, greater trust in the Lord, and joy and happiness that worldly things cannot bring. At the conclusion of my MTC experience, I wrote in my journal that I knew I had a life altering experience, even if I never set foot in the mission field. While that is certainly true, oh how little did I realize how much I would learn and grow once I did get into the mission field.

Another meaningful experience I had at the Missionary Training Center was when one of my instructors challenged us missionaries in the class to write down three personal goals that would guide us in our daily missionary efforts. The MTC instructor wrote on the chalk board: "As a missionary, I will always and without conditions: _____." and then asked us to fill in the blank.

This request came on the day when they introduced us to the Missionary Handbook, commonly called the "White Bible". So I wrote these three goals on the back page (see Figure 4):

- I will work hard
- I will be obedient
- I will love others

Daily striving to live up to these three goals served me well on my mission; it brought success, safety, and joy. Living by these goals has also brought blessings to my personal and professional life after my mission.

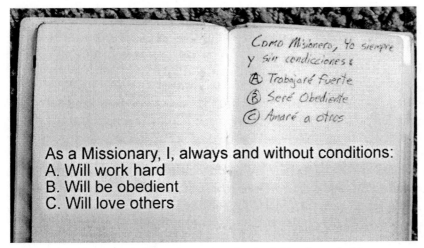

As a Missionary, I, always and without conditions:
A. Will work hard
B. Will be obedient
C. Will love others

Figure 4: A photograph of the Missionary Handbook of Elder Jimmy Smith

Goal: Work Hard

A good work ethic was something my parents always taught me to have. I can remember my father telling me a story from his mission about how he had to be in the hospital for a few days. He regretted not being able to be out on the streets working during that time. My dad encouraged me to make the most of every day on my mission by working as hard as I could. While I can't claim perfection in this area, I did, with very few exceptions, work as hard as I could each day. I attribute much of my joys and successes as a missionary to learning to work hard.

President Gordon B. Hinckley shared the following experience regarding the importance of working hard on his mission:

"I was not well when I arrived. Those first few weeks, because of illness and the opposition which we felt, I was discouraged. I wrote a letter home to my good father and said that I felt I was wasting my time and his money. He was my father and my stake president, and he was a wise and inspired man. He wrote a very short letter to me which said, 'Dear Gordon, I have your recent letter. I have only one suggestion: forget yourself and go to work.' Earlier that morning in our scripture class my companion and I had read these words of the Lord: 'Whosoever will save his life shall lose it; but whosoever shall lose his life for my sake and the gospel's, the same shall save it.' (Mark 8:35.)

"Those words of the Master, followed by my father's letter with his counsel to forget myself and go to work, went into my very being. With my father's letter in hand, I went into our bedroom in the house at 15 Wadham Road, where we lived, and got on my knees and made a pledge with the Lord. I covenanted that I would try to forget myself and lose myself in His service.

"That July day in 1933 was my day of decision. A new light came into my life and a new joy into my heart. The fog of England seemed to lift, and I saw the sunlight. I had a rich and wonderful mission experience, for which I shall ever be grateful" ("Taking the Gospel to Britain: A Declaration of Vision, Faith, Courage, and Truth," Ensign, July 1987, 7).

President Ezra Taft Benson also talked about the need for missionaries to work hard:

"I have often said one of the greatest secrets of missionary work is work! If a missionary works, he will get the Spirit; if he gets the Spirit, he will teach by the Spirit; and if he teaches by the Spirit, he will touch the hearts of the people and he will be happy. There will be no homesickness, no worrying about families, for all time and talents and interests are centered on the work of the ministry. Work, work, work—there is no satisfactory substitute, especially in missionary work" (The Teachings of Ezra Taft Benson [1988], 200).

Goal: Be Obedient

Obedience to the commandments of God and to the mission rules is a vital component of faithful missionary service. Great power comes to missionaries that are obedient, and therefore your mission leaders will stress the importance of keeping the commandments and rules in the Missionary Handbook. I know that I was protected by keeping the missionary rules, and the Lord blessed me, my companions, and our investigators in the process.

Elder Dennis B. Neuenschwander of the Seventy spoke of the importance of obeying the mission rules:

"Mission rules are important in the same way commandments are important. We all need to keep them, understanding that they give us strength, direction, and limits. The smart missionary will learn the intent of the rules and make them work for him. Your mission is a time of discipline and single-minded focus. You will be required to go without some things common to your current lifestyle: music, TV, videos, novels, even girls. There is nothing wrong with any of these things, ...but then again, there is nothing wrong with food either, unless you are fasting, in which case even a teaspoon of water is improper" (in Conference Report, Oct. 1991, 59; or Ensign, Nov. 1991, 43).

Goal: Love Others

Missionary work is one of the purest acts of love we can do for our fellow beings. We must love the people we have been called to serve in order to be effective servants of the Lord. We should give sincere friendship and treat others with love and kindness, even if they do not immediately accept the gospel.

Early in my mission, a leader shared this insight with me: if we are not having joy, then we are not doing missionary work correctly. I found that to be true. When we do missionary work out of a sincere love for our fellow beings, we enjoy it, for we are helping others receive the magnificent blessings of the gospel of Jesus Christ.

The following scriptures are what the Lord has said regarding love and missionary service.

- D&C 12:8 "And no one can assist in this work except he shall be humble and full of love, having faith, hope, and charity, being temperate in all things, whatsoever shall be entrusted to his care."
- D&C 18:15-16 "And if it so be that you should labor all your days in crying repentance unto this people, and bring, save it be one soul unto me, how great shall be your joy with him in the kingdom of my Father! And now, if your joy will be great with one soul that you have brought unto me into the kingdom of my Father, how great will be your joy if you should bring many souls unto me!"
- D&C 121:41 "No power or influence can or ought to be maintained by virtue of the priesthood, only by persuasion, by

long-suffering, by gentleness and meekness, and by love unfeigned."

As I applied those gospel principles to my missionary work, my love grew for the people of Argentina. I learned to not only show my love, but to verbally express love to my parents, my companions, and others. Many parents become pleasantly surprised when, in the letters they receive, their missionary expresses each week his or her deep love for family and other gospel blessings. Missionary work has a tendency to inspire that kind of love and appreciation.

That MTC instructor's lesson about goals was truly inspired, and those goals I set in the MTC (to work hard, be obedient, and love others) were also inspired by the Spirit of the Lord. As a missionary, you will have many rules, but perhaps the most important may be the ones you set for yourself. Work hard, obey, and love others served me well, and perhaps they will help you too. I would encourage you to think about this same question, in case one of your MTC instructors asks you to fill in the blanks: "As a missionary, I will always and without conditions do the following: _____."

Conclusion

It has been said that angels surround the MTC, protecting it with an unseen army. I don't know if that is true or not, but I do know that the MTC was a wonderful experience, and that my time there helped prepare me for the mission field. My Spanish skills, though far from fluent when I left the MTC, were good enough. Similarly, my knowledge of the missionary discussions was, in retrospect, also not perfect when I left the MTC. But my faith had been fortified, and I had learned how to draw upon the power of the Lord. And when you've learned those lessons, you are prepared to go forth, find, teach, and baptize.

May the Lord bless and be with you as you leave the Missionary Training Center and go on to your assigned mission destination. If you enter with a humble desire to learn, your MTC experience will be uplifting and fruitful. You will leave a more prepared missionary and become an effective tool the Lord can use to gather His elect.

Chapter 12   Open Your Mouth

"Is it not always easy for us to "publish the gospel among every people that (we shall) be permitted to see" (D&C 19:29) because many of us are shy, and starting a conversation with a stranger can be challenging. Yet it is one of the most important things we can do if the message is to be taken to everyone. Miracles could happen if we would just open our mouths" (Joe J. Christensen, "Open Your Mouths: The Courage to Share the Gospel," Ensign, Dec. 1981, 5–9).

One of the most important and constant tasks you must do as a missionary is to continually open your mouth. Open your mouth to testify of Jesus Christ and His Atonement. Open your mouth to give testimony of Joseph Smith and his First Vision of God the Father and His Son. Open your mouth to testify of the truthfulness of the Book of Mormon: Another Testament of Jesus Christ. To do this takes great courage, but miracles happen when missionaries do it.

Open Your Mouth: A Commandment to Missionaries

The Doctrine and Covenants is filled with scriptures commanding missionaries to open their mouths and preach the gospel. Almost always those scriptures contain a promise from the Lord that they will be blessed to know what to say if they take that step of faith and open their mouth. Here are a few:

- D&C 24:12, Oliver Cowdery is called to preach the gospel and the Lord says, "At all times, and in all places, he shall open his mouth and declare my gospel as with the voice of a trump, both day and night."

- D&C 28:16, again, to Oliver Cowdery the Lord says "And thou must open thy mouth at all times, declaring my gospel with the sound of rejoicing."
- D&C 30:11, John Whitmer is called to preach the gospel and the Lord says, "Yea, you shall ever open your mouth in my cause, not fearing what man can do, for I am with you."
- D&C 33:10, to Ezra Thayre and Northrop Sweet the Lord says it three times: verse 8 "Open your mouths and they shall be filled," verse 9 "Open your mouths and spare not," and again in verse 10 "Open your mouths and they shall be filled."
- D&C 60:2, to the Elders of the Church the Lord says, "But with some I am not well pleased, for they will not open their mouths, but they hide the talent which I have given unto them, because of the fear of man."
- D&C 71:1, to Joseph Smith and Sidney Rigdon the Lord says, "it is necessary and expedient in me that you should open your mouths in proclaiming my gospel...according to that portion of Spirit and power which shall be given unto you, even as I will."

For many missionaries this commandment to "open your mouth" is not easy, which is probably why the Lord mentions it again and again in the scriptures. Many missionaries, including myself as a young missionary, are shy and unsure of themselves. Many are called to preach the gospel in lands where they don't speak the native language. The excuses for not opening your mouth as a missionary are many but all are rooted in "the fear of man" rather than trust in God. As noted in the scriptures above, when missionaries open their mouths to declare the gospel, the Lord will be with them and help them know what to say. But it is not until missionaries take that necessary step that the Lord will use them as an instrument in his hands.

Door Knocking

One of the most common ways for missionaries around the world to open their mouths is by knocking on doors, or "tracting" as we like to call it in Mormon terminology. You've probably seen movies, whether Church-made or otherwise, depicting LDS missionaries knocking on doors and trying, usually without much luck, to strike up a conversation with the person who answers. And truthfully, this is not the most effective way to find people to teach, but if you tract prayerfully, allowing yourself to be led by the Spirit, the Lord can lead you to the right people.

One of my favorite tracting stories comes from a missionary named Bill Carpenter. I first heard his story when I was a missionary in Argentina, and it inspired me to be more prayerful and diligent in my contacting efforts.

Brother Carpenter was called on his mission to Des Moines, Iowa. The first area he was assigned to was a small city with no ward, no branch, and not even any members of the Church. He and his senior companion were sent there to open up the area. So they bought a map and prayed about what part of the city to start knocking doors. "Tracting by the spirit," Brother Carpenter called it.

They decided on a street in the north east part of the city and started knocking doors in the cold, snowy weather. They were not having much luck when they came upon a house that had been in a fire. They skipped that house, of course, because people don't live in burnt down houses, but the Spirit whispered to them to go knock on that door. So they did and a lady answered the door and invited them in.

Brother Carpenter and his companion began teaching her the first discussion and the Spirit of the Lord was being felt strongly by everyone present. To his senior companion's great surprise, Brother Carpenter asked this woman if you wanted to get baptized. And then to his trainer's even greater surprise, the woman responded that, yes, she would like to get baptized, and so would her three daughters.

Such are the miracles that occur when you have faith, open your mouth, and follow the guidance of the Spirit.

Street Contacting

In Argentina, we didn't do much door knocking. The primary way in which we opened our mouths in my mission was street contacting. Though I call it street contacting, it is not limited to only talking to people in the street. It is talking to people in everyday situations in various scenarios as you go through the day, in the street, on the bus, or wherever you cross paths with people.

In most of Argentina, the missionaries don't have cars or bikes for transportation, so everywhere we went we either walked or took the bus. This was the case for most other Argentines as well; therefore we constantly came across people throughout the day. It was difficult for me at first, to strike up a gospel conversation in the street or on the bus, but with practice, I learned to do it effectively as a missionary.

Throughout my mission it took continual effort to open my mouth in these instances, which nearly encompassed the whole day. We talked to people we passed on the side walk, or that we bumped into at the grocery store. We talked to the attendant at the photo store, or any number of other situations. Wherever you go, you wear that missionary name tag and there is no time off from being a representative of the Lord.

During my first couple of weeks in Argentina, we took the bus a lot, but I was far too shy and unsure of my Spanish language skills to sit down next to a stranger and begin a conversation about the gospel of Jesus Christ. I watched my companion do it time and time again as we rode the bus traveling to teaching appointments or on other errands.

After a week or two, my senior companion challenged me to sit down next to someone on the bus and talk to him. Reluctantly, I did it, and my first attempt was actually rather successful. The man I sat down next to was friendly and even gave me his name and phone number so we could come by his home later for more discussions. This interaction gave me additional confidence, and I continued opening my mouth to testify to strangers on the bus for the rest of my mission.

Of course not everyone we met was as nice as that first man I contacted on the bus. Many people would not talk to us, would get up and move to another seat, or tried to argue with us, though we tried not to argue back. Regardless of whether or not my testimony was received by others, I always tried to open my mouth on the bus, in the store, on the street, and in other situations to testify of the Lord Jesus Christ and of the message of the restored gospel.

If we missionaries hadn't opened our mouth and shared our message in these everyday situations, we never would have met most the people on my mission who eventually were baptized. We wouldn't have gotten to know and convert the Almada family who lived next door to us. The conversion of Juan Carlos Lopez, who we first met in the street, never would have happened without us opening our mouths. And the Godoy family, a wonderful couple with two children, was baptized after we simply opened our mouths and struck up a conversation.

Conversion of the Godoy Family

The story of how we met and baptized the Godoy family is a perfect example of how the Lord is preparing people to receive the gospel and all missionaries have to do is have the courage to open their mouths.

My companion and I met the Godoy family in the city of Rosario Argentina. Carlos and his wife, Beatriz, were at a photo shop, with their two children, Carlos Jr. and Angelica, getting a family photo made. My companion and I walked into the store right at that moment, and while we waited for the attendant to help us, we commented on what a cute family they were. The Godoy's were friendly and we chatted for a minute, but we really didn't talk about the gospel before they had to leave.

The next day, we were visiting a member at his work and we just happened to run into Carlos Godoy again. This time we did talk to him about the gospel, and he seemed eager to learn more. We asked if we could come to his home to teach a discussion to his family, and we set the appointment for a few days later.

When we arrived at the Godoy's home for the first discussion, we found their extremely modest home in pristine condition. We could tell they really made an effort to clean and beautify their home in preparation for our visit. We sat down with the whole family around the kitchen table and talked about the gospel of Jesus Christ, Heavenly Father's plan of happiness, the restoration of the gospel through Joseph Smith, and the Book of Mormon. The Godoy's were eager learners, and they seemed from the beginning to be a "golden" family.

We scheduled the second discussion, and that lesson went very well. We invited them to be baptized, and they said they wanted to. Unfortunately, though, we found out that they were not legally married, which meant they couldn't get baptized until that happened. Carlos and Beatriz had been together since high school, but due to the expense and other factors, they had never been legally married. When 8-year-old Angelica heard that they couldn't get baptized until her parents got married, she exclaimed, "Casense Ya!" (Get married already!).

So the Godoy's immediately planned their wedding. My companion and I attended the civil marriage at city hall, and then they held a grand wedding party. The following Sunday, July 13, 1997, the entire Godoy family got baptized. It was a wonderful occasion to see this beautiful family get baptized and start down the path to eternal life together.

In his earlier years, Carlos drank and made other mistakes. Carlos' repentance was thorough and sincere, and he was so happy to be baptized and have a new, clean start on life. Beatriz was also very happy to see her entire family get baptized together; she loves her family a great deal. Little Carlos said he got a little nervous prior to his baptism, but when he saw his dad and mom do it, he was very excited to get baptized himself. And as for little Angelica, what else can I say except she truly was a little angel.

Meeting and baptizing this family was one of many cases on my mission in which the Lord did all the work. All my companion and I had to do was be in the right place at the right time, open our mouths, and let the Lord fill it. We were so blessed to meet the Godoy family and see them become members of God's kingdom on earth. And I can't wait to see them again, whether it be in this life or the next.

Figure 5: Elder Josh Brown, Carlos Godoy, Carlos Godoy Jr., Elder Jimmy Smith, Angelica Godoy, and Beatriz Godoy at a church building in Rosario, Argentina.

Conclusion

"Verily I say unto you, lift up your voices unto this people; speak the thoughts that I shall put into your hearts, and you shall not be confounded before men; For it shall be given you in the very hour, yea, in the very moment, what ye shall say." (D&C 100: 5-6) I testify that this is true. Open your mouth every chance you get and testify of the Lord and his restored Church and the gospel message that you carry as a missionary. If you do, the Lord will bless you with the right words, and he will guide you to the right people. The Spirit will penetrate the hearts of your listeners and testify of the truthfulness of your words. You will be blessed and the Lord will be able to bless many others as you become an instrument in his hands to bring souls unto Christ.

Chapter 13   The Name Tag

"Respect the title you hold. There are few men in the Church who are referred to as "Elder," but one is you—a full-time missionary. Respect that title; refer to it with reverence. Many men have brought honor to it... You do the same." (Dennis B. Neuenschwander, "To a Missionary Son," October 1991)

The Mormon missionary name tag or badge is one of the most recognizable visual features of our missionaries. When you get baptized, you take upon yourself the name of Christ (see D&C 20:37). Once you become a missionary, you literally take upon yourself the name of Jesus Christ through the name tag, your words, and your deeds.

On the one hand, the missionary badge is simply a name tag, but on the other hand, it is symbolic of the work missionaries have been called to do. The name tag is a constant reminder, to themselves and to all who see them, of who missionaries are and who and what they represent. It is a symbol of the Church they represent and of the Savior whose messengers they are.

My Missionary Commission

Elder Bruce R. McConkie spoke about the commission missionaries are given. A commission has several meanings, most of which are very applicable to missionaries of The Church of Jesus Christ of Latter-day Saints. According to Webster's dictionary, a commission means:

- *"An authorization or command to perform prescribed acts."*
  Missionaries have been given the authority to preach the

gospel. The Lord has said that anyone "embracing this calling and commandment, shall be ordained and sent forth to preach the everlasting gospel among the nations" (D&C 36:5).

- *"Authority to act for, in behalf of, or in place of another."* Missionaries have been commissioned to act in the place of the Savior, for they are representatives of Jesus Christ and His Church. "What I the Lord have spoken...whether by mine own voice or by the voice of my servants, it is the same" (D&C 1:38).
- *"A group of persons directed to perform some duty."* Missionaries have been entrusted with very important tasks and duties. "And this gospel shall be preached unto every nation, and kindred, and tongue, and people" (D&C 133:37).

The name tag is a sign of the commission missionaries have been given. Elder Bruce R. McConkie, in an address he delivered while serving as president of the Australian Mission from 1961 to 1964, explained the missionary's commission this way:

I am called of God. My authority is above that of the kings of the earth. By revelation I have been selected as a personal representative of the Lord Jesus Christ. He is my Master and He has chosen me to represent Him. To stand in His place, to say and do what He himself would say and do if He personally were ministering to the very people to whom He has sent me. My voice is His voice, and my acts are His acts; my words are His words and my doctrine is His doctrine. My commission is to do what He wants done. To say what He wants said. To be a living modern witness in word and deed of the divinity of His great and marvelous latter-day work.

One Sister Missionary's Name Tag

Elder Robert L. Simpson once spoke about the power and influence one sister missionary had by simply wearing her name tag and faithfully performing her service.

"Few are aware of the pure Christian service being administered at refugee camps in Thailand and in the Philippines by our missionary sisters. Basically, these sisters are restricted to teaching the English language and Western culture, but there is a deeper teaching that takes place through their pure love and sweet attitude toward these displaced people.

The story is told of a young camp refugee from Cambodia who was relocated in California. He found his way into one of our Church meetinghouses because the name of the Church on the sign out front corresponded with the one he used to look at each day on the name tag of the wonderful missionary sister who taught him at the camp. People don't soon forget acts of simple kindness. Pure love can transcend all differences" (Robert L. Simpson, "The Simplicity of Gospel Truths," Ensign May 1984).

An Outward Sign of Identity

Finally, here is another reminder about the importance of the missionary name tag from Sister Susan W. Tanner, former General Young Women's President for the Church.

"Has your mother or father ever reminded you as you were leaving the house to 'remember who you are'? What do they mean by that? 'Remember that you are part of this family, with a reputation to uphold.' And, even more importantly, 'remember that you are a child of God and must act accordingly.' Missionaries wear a badge as a constant reminder that they are representatives of The Church of Jesus Christ of Latter-day Saints. This reminds missionaries to dress modestly and comely, to treat people with politeness, and to strive to have Christ's image in their countenances. They must do these things because they wear that name tag, an outward sign of their identity" (Susan W. Tanner, "Daughters of Heavenly Father," Ensign May 2007).

Conclusion: How to Become an Effective Missionary

Throughout this section, we have discussed many ways to prepare spiritually to become an effective missionary and a powerful instrument in the hands of the Lord. Let's briefly review them.

- *Stay worthy*. Worthiness is a pre-requisite to missionary work. You will need to be worthy to have the companionship of the Spirit to guide you in your mission preparation and in your missionary work.

- **Know and use the scriptures**, especially The Book of Mormon. If you haven't yet, start reading the scriptures daily, and pray to God for your own testimony of their truthfulness.
- **The MTC.** Go there spiritually minded, utilize your time wisely, and you will come away a much more prepared and effective missionary.
- **Open your mouth.** As missionaries, you must open your mouth at all times and in all places to find the people the Lord would have you teach. Young people can practice this now by talking to their non-member friends about the gospel.
- **The name tag** missionaries wear has two names on it: their own and the Savior's. The tag can remind you who you are and who you represent. Young people can learn the gospel and come closer to the Lord so they can better represent Him.

Brothers and sisters, as you strive now and throughout your mission to become proficient in what you do, represent the Lord and preach His gospel, the Lord will bless you. The Lord will recognize your efforts, strengthen you, and guide you. You will then become an effective missionary of the Lord and you'll play a vital role in bringing souls unto Christ and building the kingdom of God.

Section V. Additional Blessings of Missionary Work

Chapter 14 Seventeen Blessings of Missionary Service

"Missionary work, like the tithing, will pour out blessings, as Malachi said, so many blessings that there'll hardly be room enough to receive them (See Mal. 3:10.)" (Spencer W. Kimball, Area Conference Report, Korea, Aug. 1975, p. 61).

As we approach the end of the book, I'd like to spend a little more time talking about the blessings that come to us when we participate in missionary work. Elder Carlos E. Asay, former member of the First Quorum of the Seventy and Presidency of the Seventy, gave a talk on the blessings of sharing the gospel.

"Perhaps your desire or will to serve would increase if you understood more fully the blessings associated with missionary service. God often reveals commandments and blessings together. For example, he gave the Word of Wisdom listing the commandments, and, at the same time, he recited a number of blessings that those who obeyed the commandments would receive. I would like to discuss with you some of the blessings associated with full-time missionary service. I can't list everything, for there are so many blessings that I cannot number them, but I will share those that appear to be most common."

1. *Eternal Life*: "And every one that hath forsaken houses, or brethren, or sisters, or father, or mother, or wife, or children, or lands, for my name's sake, shall receive an hundredfold, and shall inherit everlasting life." (Matt. 19:29)

95

2. *Leadership Training*: "Returned missionaries provide valuable leadership in the Church, especially in the developing countries of the world."
3. *Building the Kingdom; Preparing a People for Christ's Second Coming*: "Wherefore, may the kingdom of God go forth, that the kingdom of heaven may come." (D&C 65:2, 6.)
4. *Memorable Experiences*: "President Kimball has referred to missionary service as high adventure. He did so because the work is stirring and exciting."
5. *Establishing Abiding Friendships*: "The friendships we establish in the mission field with companions and converts become eternal."
6. *Developing Love and Understanding of People*: "Missionaries gain a love and understanding of others through their service."
7. *Rendering Service*: "He doth require that ye should do as he hath commanded you; for which if ye do, he doth immediately bless you." (Mosiah 2: 23–24.)
8. *Being a Peacemaker*: Elder N. Eldon Tanner said: "If every member of this Church would accept the call of our prophet today ...and become missionaries in very deed, we could contribute more to the cause of peace than all the power that might be gathered together by all the governments." (Conference Report, Oct. 1962, p. 69)
9. *Developing and Polishing Character*: Stephen L Richards, formerly of the Quorum of the Twelve Apostles, talked about the influence of missions upon the Latter-day Saints. "The fundamental character of our manhood and womanhood has been improved," he said.
10. *Forgiveness of Sins*: Elder George F. Richards, also a former member of the Quorum of the Twelve, said: "In the name of the Lord I want to promise you that in the acceptance of the mission call and the dedication of yourself to the work, the Lord will forgive you of past transgressions."
11. *Growth of Testimony*: "Missionaries teach and testify... Each time they do, they invite the Spirit, and the truths they proclaim become more and more deeply ingrained in their own souls."
12. *Companionship of the Holy Spirit*: "Of all the companionships established in the mission field, the most cherished is the companionship of the Holy Spirit."
13. *Closeness to the Lord*: "For how knoweth a man the master whom he has not served?" (Mosiah 5:13.) "No one will ever

fully understand the Savior's work until he has invested in the business of saving souls, for that was the Savior's role."

14. **Growth in Faith**: Mission "experiences plant seeds of faith in their hearts."

15. **Growth in Knowledge of the Gospel**: "missions are schools of gospel learning, even schools for the prophets."

16. **Peace of Conscience**: Elder George Albert Smith taught that missionary work brings "peace and happiness beyond all understanding." (Conference Report, Apr. 1922, p. 53.)

17. **Joy**: President Heber J. Grant testified: "[I] had more joy while in the mission field than ever before or since."(Improvement Era, Oct. 1936, p. 659.)

"I have given you seventeen blessings that result from missionary service. There are more—the list is almost endless. Please understand that these blessings and more can be yours, if you become converted to the service and make yourselves available to respond" (Carlos E. Asay, "The Blessings of Sharing the Gospel," Prospective Missionary Conference in Provo, Utah, September 1984).

I know that missionary service requires sacrifice, but I also know that "sacrifice brings forth the blessings of heaven" ("Praise to the Man," Hymns, no. 27). I add my testimony to Elder Asay's, that as you faithfully serve a full-time mission, the blessings of the Lord will be poured out upon you. You and your family will receive blessings of both temporal and spiritual nature which will grant you joy in this life and in the eternities.

Chapter 15   Temples and Temple Marriage

"May the Lord bless you to go forward humbly, prayerfully, and worthily to the mission field and serve as instruments in bringing many souls to him. Know clearly that there are hundreds of thousands who have done so, who have served and are serving faithfully and worthily in the work of the Lord. While you are young, set a pattern of worthiness and faithful service. Do so with all of your heart, and the Lord will greatly bless you, not only in the mission field, but through the rest of your life, your temple marriage, and right into the eternities" (Gene R. Cook, "Worthy to Serve," New Era, May 1994).

The final blessings of missionary work I'd like to mention are those that come from the temple, the House of the Lord. Missionary work and temple blessing are integrally related. Temples bless the lives of all members, and a mission helps prepare young people for eternal marriage and the highest blessings of the temple. Understanding the role of temples in our religion can also help prepare you to be a better missionary.

Temples Integral to Missionary Work

Temples are an integral part of missionary work for a couple of reasons: 1) The temple endowment gives missionaries power from on high to do their work. 2) Baptism, which is the main goal of missionary work, is the first step toward higher ordinances of salvation received in the temple.

Temple Endowment Gives Missionaries Power

New missionaries generally go to the temple to receive their endowment just a few weeks prior to leaving on their mission. Through the endowment and other temple ordinances, missionaries receive knowledge, power, and strength that comes through a greater understanding of Heavenly Father's plan.

The word "endowment," strictly speaking, refers to a gift. In the case of the temple endowment, it is a gift of knowledge, instructions, and covenants that allow the faithful to return to live with God. President Brigham Young gave this definition of the endowment: "Your endowment is to receive all those ordinances in the house of the Lord, which are necessary for you, after you have departed this life, to enable you to walk back to the presence of the Father" (Discourses of Brigham Young, sel. John A. Widtsoe, p. 416).

Many modern prophets and apostles have taught the importance of receiving the temple endowment prior to serving a mission. President Howard W. Hunter, 14th president of the Church, said: "Let us prepare every missionary to go to the temple worthily and to make that experience an even greater highlight than receiving the mission call" (Conference Report, October 1994, 118).

Elder Jeffrey R. Holland has said:

"Going to the temple for your own endowment . . . [is] an integral part of your mission preparation. . . . [You should] understand the significance of those temple covenants [and] the inextricable link between your endowment and your missionary success. Indeed, the very word endowment conveys the essence of that vital link. An endowment is a gift. You cannot do this work alone. We have to have heaven's help, we have to have the 'gifts' of God. . . . This work is so serious and the adversary's opposition to it so great that we need every divine power to enhance our effort and move the Church steadily forward" ('Making and Keeping Covenants,' missionary satellite broadcast, Apr. 25, 1997).

Elder Bruce R. McConkie said this of the temple endowment and missionary work:

"The apostles—or any ministers or missionaries in any age— are not fully qualified to go forth, preach the gospel, and build up the kingdom, unless they have the gift of the Holy Ghost and also are endowed with power from on high, meaning [they] have received certain knowledge, powers, and special blessings, normally given only in the Lord's Temple" (Doctrinal New Testament Commentary, 3 vols. [1966–73], 1:859).

President Joseph Fielding Smith, 10th president of the Church said:

"Do you understand why our missionaries go to the temple before they are set apart for their mission fields? This is a requirement made of them. . . He called all the missionaries to Kirtland in the early day of the Church to receive endowments in the temple erected there. He said this was so that they could go out with greater power from on high and with greater protection" (Doctrines of Salvation, compiled by Bruce R. McConkie, 3 vols. [1954–56], 2:255).

I hope you see how vital the temple endowment is to your success as a missionary. It is a great blessing for missionaries to be able to take part in the temple ordinances prior to embarking on their missionary service. Once your mission departure date gets close, within   six months or year, you may want to think about taking the Church's Temple Preparation class through your ward or stake. Proper mission prep includes being prepared to receive and understand the temple endowment, covenants, and ordinances received there.

Baptism is the Gate to Higher Ordinances

As missionaries, your primary objective is to bring souls unto Christ by finding, teaching, and baptizing. Elder Dallin H. Oaks said:

"The purpose of our missionary work is to help the children of God fulfill a condition prescribed by our Savior and Redeemer. We preach and teach in order to baptize the children of God so that they can be saved in the celestial kingdom instead of being limited to a lesser kingdom. We do missionary work in order to baptize and confirm. That is the doctrinal basis of missionary work" (Dallin H. Oaks, "Why Do We Do Missionary Work?," New Era, Sept. 2009, 2–3).

The prophet Nephi teaches us in the Book of Mormon that baptism isn't the end, but the beginning of the journey.

"For the gate by which ye should enter is repentance and baptism by water...And then are ye in this strait and narrow path which leads to eternal life; yea, ye have entered in by the gate...And now, my beloved brethren, after ye have gotten into this strait and narrow path, I would ask if all is done? Behold, I say unto you, Nay" (2 Nephi 31: 17-19).

Baptism is the first step toward higher ordinances received at the temple. Elder David A. Bednar, in his General Conference address in May 2009, explained that "the baptismal covenant clearly contemplates a future event or events and looks forward to the temple." Quoting Elder Neal A. Maxwell, he says, "Clearly, when we baptize, our eyes should gaze beyond the baptismal font to the holy temple."

Quoting Elder Dallin H. Oaks, Elder Bednar continues and says that when we partake of the sacrament each week, "we do not witness that we take upon us the name of Jesus Christ. [Rather], we witness that we are willing to do so. The fact that we only witness to our willingness suggests that something else must happen before we actually take that sacred name upon us in the [ultimate and] most important sense." Elder Bednar goes on to explain that it is in the temple that we more fully take upon us the name of Christ (David A. Bednar, "Honorably Hold a Name and Standing," Ensign May 2009).

Elder Russell M. Nelson also taught this principle, that baptism points us to the higher ordinances of the temple when he said that "missionary work is only the beginning" of the gathering of Israel.

"The fulfillment, the consummation, of those blessings comes as those who have entered the waters of baptism perfect their lives to the point that they may enter the holy temple. Receiving an endowment there seals members of the Church to the Abrahamic covenant" (Perfection Pending, and Other Favorite Discourses [1998], 207).

My experience, in attending the temple and in baptizing families as a step toward the temple, has been that the doctrine above is true. As a new missionary, I was better able to teach the gospel because I had been blessed with the knowledge, power, and strength that comes through the greater understanding of Heavenly Father's plan as learned in the temple. Several of the families I baptized on my mission eventually went to the temple to be sealed together for time and all eternity. It was the sweetest pleasure of my mission to hear that a family that I had taught and baptized would be together forever through the power of the priesthood and the temple ordinances that bind families together on earth and in heaven. In fact the first family I baptized, the Almada family, had been sealed in the temple before my mission was complete.

Conversion and Temple Sealing of the Almada Family

The city of Paraná, Argentina, was where I was assigned as a brand new missionary. Within a week of my arrival in the city, the Almada family moved into the home right behind our apartment. Their family consisted of Fabian, the husband, Silvina, the wife, and they had four kids. With them living right behind us, our paths crossed often. I can remember my companion, Elder Loesener, often kicking the soccer ball with their oldest son as we came and went from our apartment.

Within a week or two of first meeting the Almada family, we got home one evening and were contemplating what to cook ourselves for dinner. Elder Loesener wanted to cook something that required sugar, but we didn't have any. He thought we should ask the Almada's if we could borrow some sugar. He also thought this was the perfect time to more formally meet the family and tell them about our message as missionaries for the Lord Jesus Christ. We borrowed the sugar and ended up having a nice conversation with them, and they agreed to have us come back to teach them the first discussion.

The first discussion went very well, and we scheduled the second discussion. Fabian was very interested in our message. He read the Book of Mormon and the other Church materials we gave him. He was eager to learn, asked many questions, and demonstrated great faith, dedication and determination to begin a new life with his family. At the end of the second discussion, when my companion asked them if they would be baptized, both Fabian and Silvina said yes without hesitation.

Fabian worked at night at a local panadería (bakery). One morning, after we had begun teaching the family, we awoke to find a bag of warm bread and pastries by our front door. It was so delicious, hot and fresh, we couldn't help but gobble up all the pastries. And the bread was great for sandwiches that evening and even for French toast the following morning. We began to find the bread and pastries on our door step several times a week, and we were very grateful to Fabian for thinking of us.

The Almada's were doing great. They were coming to church and progressing in the gospel. They had been searching for the true gospel of Jesus Christ and recognized it when they found it. When we taught them the Word of Wisdom, Fabian had his son go to the kitchen, get all the wine and dump it down the drain immediately. They were every missionary's dream of a golden family.

Then, about a week before their baptism, Fabian lost his job at the bakery. The economic situation was tough in Argentina at that time. Many people were without work. We knew this would be a great trial to the Almada's growing faith in the gospel, and we were amazed at how they responded. Silvina told us that the morning after Fabian lost his job he knelt and prayed fervently for 30 minutes. Afterwards he arose and headed out the door with a determination to find work to provide for his family.

Not only did Fabian offer a prayer, but his wife and children and we missionaries were all praying that he would find a job. We thought it would take days or weeks for Fabian to find something, but the Lord answered our prayers very rapidly. Fabian came home that very night with not just one job, but two jobs, which was a tremendous blessing. He was going to be able to work more hours and get more pay than he had before. It was a true miracle.

On February 8, 1996, we held the baptismal service for the Almada family. I baptized Fabian and their 10-year-old son Cristian. Elder

Loesener baptized Silvina and Anai, their 8-year-old daughter. It was a wonderful experience for all.

Following the baptisms, as traditional in LDS baptismal services, there were additional talks once the family had dried off and gotten dressed. My companion was conducting and, to my surprise, he asked Fabian to come to the front and bear his testimony. I thought it was a bold move, but Elder Loesener must have been prompted by the Spirit. Fabian stood up and confidently bore a powerful testimony of the restored gospel of Jesus Christ.

Not many days later, I was transferred out of that city, but Elder Loesener later told me about the Almadas' temple sealing. He said that they began immediately to save up money for a trip to the temple. They served faithfully in the Church over the next year. Then at a great cost and sacrifice, a year after their baptism, the Almadas took a bus to the Buenos Aires temple and their family was sealed together. Elder Loesener, an Argentine native, was home from his mission by that time and was able to attend the ceremony.

When Fabian Almada lost his job, his convictions in his new found faith were not shaken. He, along with his family and friends, prayed in faith, and with great power the Lord answered and poured out blessings, both temporal and spiritual, upon the Almada family. Now they have been sealed by the priesthood power and have entered into covenants that will allow them, according to their faithfulness, to return to live with Heavenly Father.

This is what missionary work is all about: helping families come unto Christ and begin the journey that will take them to the Lord's temple to have eternal blessings sealed upon them. May you, as a missionary, always remain worthy of the temple blessings. And may you have great power and success in helping families take the first steps towards the blessings of the holy temple.

Missions and Temple Marriage

One other thing I'd like to discuss concerning missionary work and temples is that a mission prepares you in many ways for your future temple marriage. Learning to work together and get along with your mission companion is excellent practice for learning to be a good spouse and eternal companion.

Those men and women who are sealed in the temple have the assurance that their marriage will continue forever if they obey their covenants. They know that nothing, not even death, can permanently separate them.

The 16th president of the Church, Thomas S. Monson, said: "Make certain that the marriage in your future is a temple marriage. There is no scene so sweet, no time so sacred as that very special day of your marriage. Then and there you glimpse celestial joy. Be alert; do not permit temptation to rob you of this blessing" (Whom Shall I Marry?, New Era, Oct. 2004).

Heber J. Grant, 7th president of the Church, emphasized the importance of every young man and woman starting their life together with a temple marriage.

"I believe that no worthy young Latter-day Saint man or woman should spare any reasonable effort to come to a house of the Lord to begin life together. ...The blessings and promises that come from beginning life together, for time and eternity, in a temple of the Lord, cannot be obtained in any other way and worthy young Latter-day Saint men and women who so begin life together find that their eternal partnership under the everlasting covenant becomes the foundation upon which are built peace, happiness, virtue, love, and all of the other eternal verities of life, here and hereafter" (Heber J. Grant, "Beginning Life Together," Improvement Era, Apr. 1936, pp. 198–99).

Jacob's Efforts to Marry in the Covenant

The story of Jacob marrying Rachel has always seemed a good example of making every possible effort for a temple marriage. When Jacob was ready to get married, his father, Isaac, instructed him not to marry any of the daughters of Canaan because they were not of their faith. Rather, Isaac instructed Jacob to go to his uncle Laban's home and seek a wife there, among people of their same faith (see Genesis 27 & 28).

So great was Jacob's desire to marry someone of his faith that he traveled a long distance to meet Rachel, the daughter of Laban. They met at a well, fell in love, and Laban promised they could get married if Jacob would complete seven years of service. The Bible records that, "Jacob served seven years for Rachel; and they seemed unto him but a few days, for the love he had to her" (Genesis 29: 20).

A Mission Prepares You for Temple Marriage

We know that temple marriage is beautiful and an essential ordinance in order to receive exaltation in the Celestial Kingdom of Our Heavenly Father (see D&C 131:2). Faithfully serving a mission will help prepare young men and young women for that temple sealing. Elder Richard G. Scott taught that mission "experiences will develop a foundation for the later blessing of your being a strong husband and father." He further said:

"Now may I speak from my heart of what an honorable full-time mission has meant to me personally…I fell in love with an exceptional young woman. At a critical point in our courtship, she made it very clear that she would only be married in the temple to a returned missionary. Duly motivated, I served a mission in Uruguay. It was not easy. The Lord gave me many challenges that became stepping-stones to personal growth. There I gained my testimony that God the Father and His Beloved Son, Jesus Christ, did in fact visit Joseph Smith to begin a restoration of truth, priesthood authority, and the true Church on earth…At the same time, my future eternal companion, Jeanene, was being molded to become an exceptional wife and mother by her own mission. Most important, all that I now hold dear in life began to mature in the mission field. Had I not been encouraged to be a missionary, I would not have the eternal companion or precious family I dearly love" (Richard G. Scott, "Now Is the Time to Serve a Mission! Elder," Ensign May 2006).

My Temple Marriage

I know that my faithful missionary service helped prepare me for a temple marriage. It helped me learn to get along with others and to work together for common goals. My mission helped me grow spiritually and provided a foundation for having a Christ-centered life along with my wife. I love my wife with all my heart, and I am eternally grateful that we started off our marriage the right way, being sealed by priesthood authority in the Lord's temple. I know that as you strive to do your duty as a missionary, the Lord will bless you with a stronger marriage, and a happier life on earth and in heaven.

Figure 6: Jimmy and Heather Smith on their wedding day in front of the Mount Timpanogos temple

Chapter 16 Concluding Remarks

"May God bless each one of you. You are so precious to us. We, the Brethren, are overwhelmed with the goodness of the youth of the Church. Everywhere I go, in every stake, I see faces like yours; what a reassurance that is to me, for I think that we are in good hands... Resolve what you have to do to be better and leave this great auditorium today with this commitment: "Heavenly Father, I will be ready in every way—spiritually, physically, emotionally—for whatever it is that thou wouldst have me do in the building of thy Kingdom on the earth" (M. Russell Ballard, "You— the Leaders in 1988," Ensign, Mar. 1979, 69–73).

Brothers and Sisters, the blessings of missionary work are truly great, for both the missionary and the people he or she touches. For the missionary, it is a time of spiritual growth and maturity. I have seen it time and time again: A boy leaves on his mission with a modest testimony of the gospel, and he returns home a man, with leadership skills, and strong desires to continue serving in the Lord's vineyard.

For the people that you teach as a missionary, this work will bless their lives and bring them peace, joy, and eternal life if they are faithful. Even if you don't baptize a single soul, your mission can still be successful. Take the prophet Abinadi of the Book of Mormon as an example. In his missionary preaching to the people of King Noah, Abinadi died without knowing if anyone believed his teachings. But Alma heard his testimony and was converted, and he eventually became a great prophet. Because of Abinadi's efforts, Alma and his descendants became a powerful influence for good with the Nephite civilization for many generations.

You Cannot Foretell the Effects of Missionary Work

My great grandmother lived in Georgia, in the early 1900s at the time when Charles A. Callis served as mission president there. Elder Callis was a member of the Quorum of the Twelve Apostles from 1933-1947, but prior to that he served as president of the Southern States Mission for nearly thirty years. He had a great impact upon the Saints in the south, so much so that my great grandmother named my grandfather, Callis Thompson, after him.

President Gordon B. Hinckley once told a story that was relayed to him from Elder Callis about some of the unseen benefits of missionary work. Said President Hinckley to a group of missionaries:

"You don't know how much good you can do; you can't foresee the results of the effort you put in. Years ago, President Charles A. Callis, then a member of the Quorum of the Twelve, but who previously was president of the Southern States Mission for twenty-five years, told me this story. He said that he had a missionary in the southern [United States] who came in to get his release at the conclusion of his mission. His mission president said to him, 'Have you had a good mission?'

"He said, 'No.'

" 'How is that?'

"'Well, I haven't had any results from my work. I have wasted my time and my father's money. It's been a waste of time.'

"Brother Callis said, 'Haven't you baptized anyone?'

"He said, 'I baptized only one person during the two years that I have been here. That was a twelve-year-old boy up in the back hollows of Tennessee.'

"He went home with a sense of failure. Brother Callis said, 'I decided to follow that boy who had been baptized. I wanted to know what became of him. ...

"... 'I followed him through the years. He became the Sunday School Superintendent, and he eventually became the branch president. He married. He moved off the little tenant farm on which he and his parents before him had lived and got a piece of ground of his own and made it fruitful. He became the district president. He sold that piece of ground in Tennessee and moved to Idaho and bought a farm along the Snake River and prospered there. His children grew. They went on missions. They came home. They had children of their own who went on missions.'

"Brother Callis continued, 'I've just spent a week up in Idaho looking up every member of that family that I could find and talking to them about their missionary service. I discovered that, as the result of the baptism of that one little boy in the back hollows of Tennessee by a missionary who thought he had failed, more than 1,100 people have come into the Church.'

"You never can foretell the consequences of your work, my beloved brethren and sisters, when you serve as missionaries" (Teachings of Gordon B. Hinckley [1997], 360–61).

Like Elder Ballard said in the quote at the beginning of this final chapter, I hope that after reading this book, you have a firm resolve to go and prepare yourself in every way, "spiritually, physically, emotionally," to answer the call to build the Kingdom of God on earth by being a full-time missionary. I hope you have been taught, inspired, and given information to help in that preparation. If you have questions about preparing for your mission, first talk to your parents, and then talk your local priesthood leaders. After that, if you need further help, please feel free to reach out to me.

Find my contact information on my website
www.MormonMissionPrep.com/contact/

My mission was a wonderful experience. I grew in ways that otherwise would not have happened. My mission was not easy, in fact it was quite challenging at times. But during my mission, I grew closer to the Lord. I learned to rely on His Spirit to guide me, and my testimony of our Savior and the restored gospel of Jesus Christ became strengthened.

During my mission I was able to meet, teach, and baptize many individuals and families. Finding people who are eager to learn the gospel and teaching them the truths of eternity brought me great joy. In fact, there is no greater happiness than to see a family enter into the waters of baptism, then continue on the gospel path that will lead to eternal life.

I know that we are children of a Heavenly Father. God our Eternal Father loves us. He sent His Son to show us the way. Jesus Christ is the Savior. He died for our sins, and He rose again on the third day. He lives today and guides our Church through a living prophet. Joseph Smith truly was a prophet, and the Book of Mormon is the word of God. The priesthood has been restored, and the keys of the priesthood are only found in The Church of Jesus Christ of Latter-day Saints.

I know these things are true, and I know the world needs to know these truths. The gospel of Jesus Christ blesses lives. If you believe these things to be true, the Lord needs you to be part of His missionary force. May the Lord bless you in your mission preparation and in your missionary service.

Appendix 1: LDS Talks on Missionary Work

Our prophets, apostles, and general authorities have given many great talks on the topic of missionary preparation. Here are just a few that I recommend you read:

- *Preparing the World for the Second Coming* by Elder Neil L. Andersen, April, 2011
- *As We Meet Together Again* by President Thomas S. Monson, Oct., 2010
- *Be Thou an Example of the Believers* by Elder Russell M. Nelson, Oct., 2010
- *The Divine Call of a Missionary* by Elder Ronald A. Rasband, April, 2010
- *I Love Loud Boys* by Elder Yoon Hwan Choi, Oct., 2009
- *Raising the Bar* by Elder L. Tom Perry, Nov., 2007
- Special Missionary Preparation Issue of New Era, March, 2007
- *The Five M's of Missionary Work*, by President Thomas S. Monson, March, 2007
- *Your Mission Will Change Everything* by Elder David F. Evans, April, 2006
- *Now Is the Time to Serve a Mission!* by Elder Richard G. Scott, April, 2006
- *Becoming a Missionary* by Elder David A. Bednar, Oct., 2005
- *One More Young Man* by Elder M. Russell Ballard, April, 2005
- *The Power of Preach My Gospel* by Elder Richard G. Scott, April, 2005
- *Raising the Greatest Generation of Missionaries* by Elder M. Russell Ballard, May, 2003, BYU Women's Conference
- *Preparing for Missionary Service* by Elder Daryl H. Garn, April, 2003
- *To Men of the Priesthood* by President Gordon B. Hinckley, Oct., 2002
- *Greatest Generation of Missionaries* by Elder M. Russell Ballard, Oct., 2002
- *I'll Go Where You Want Me to Go* by Elder Dallin H. Oaks, Oct., 2002
- *The Returned Missionary* by Elder L. Tom Perry, Oct., 2001
- *The MTC Experience*, New Era, June, 2000
- *It's Your Call* by Barbara Jean Jones, New Era, June, 2000

- *Find the Lambs, Feed the Sheep* by President Gordon B. Hinckley, April, 1999
- *"As for Me and My House, We Will Serve the Lord"* by Elder H. Bryan Richards, Oct., 1998
- *Some Thoughts on Temples, Retention of Converts, and Missionary Service* by President Gordon B. Hinckley, Oct., 1997
- *What I Want My Son to Know before He Leaves on His Mission* by President James E. Faust, April, 1996
- *To a Missionary Son* by Dennis B. Neuenschwander, Oct., 1991
- *The Power of Commitment* by Elder M. Russell Ballard, Oct., 1989
- *Magnify Your Calling* by President Gordon B. Hinckley, April, 1989
- *Flooding the Earth with the Book of Mormon* by President Ezra Taft Benson, Oct., 1988
- *To the "Youth of the Noble Birthright"* by President Ezra Taft Benson, April, 1986
- *The Question of a Mission* by President Gordon B. Hinckley, April, 1986
- *Trust in the Lord* by Elder Gene R. Cook, March, 1986
- *The Blessings of Sharing the Gospel* by Elder Carlos E. Asay, September, 1984
- *President Kimball Speaks Out on Being a Missionary* by President Spencer W. Kimball, April, 1981
- *You—the Leaders in 1988* by Elder M. Russell Ballard, March, 1978
- *When the World Will Be Converted* by Spencer W. Kimball, Oct., 1974
- *Planning for a Full and Abundant Life* by Spencer W. Kimball, April, 1974
- *Advice to a Young Man: Now Is the Time to Prepare* by Spencer W. Kimball, June, 1973

Links to these talks, and more, can be found at
www.MormonMissionPrep.com/recommended-reading

Index of Book

ABOUT THE AUTHOR

Jimmy Smith served a mission for the LDS Church in Rosario, Argentina from 1995 to 1997. He has worked for the LDS Church since 2008 in the IT department and with Seminaries and Institutes of Religion. Jimmy specializes in Web analytics and Internet marketing. He has a bachelor's degree from Brigham Young University and an MBA degree from Arizona State University. His professional experience also includes work as a Software Engineer with Motorola and a Strategic Marketing Analyst with FedEx. He resides in Lehi, Utah, with his kind and beautiful wife Heather and their five children.